Development,
Geography, and
Economic Theory

The Ohlin Lectures

Development, Geography, and Economic Theory

Paul Krugman

The MIT Press
Cambridge, Massachusetts
London, England

This book was set in Palatino by Compset and was printed and bound in the United States of America.

Library of Congress Cataloging-in-Publication Data

Krugman, Paul R.
  Development, geography, and economic theory / Paul Krugman.
      p.   cm. — (The Ohlin lectures ; 6)
  Includes bibliographical references (p.) and index.
  ISBN 0-262-11203-5 (hc : alk. paper)
  1. Development economics—History. 2. Economic geography—
—History. I. Title. II. Series.
HD75.K79   1995   95-17955
338.9—dc20   CIP

Contents

Preface

This book consists of heavily revised versions of the Ohlin lectures that I gave at the Stockholm School of Economics in the fall of 1992.

Invitations to give lectures of this kind are, of course, a great honor. They are also a special privilege for those of us who occasionally find that we have things to say that fit awkwardly into the usual media of professional communication—ideas that are too fuzzy for a journal article, too slight for a book, yet presume too much knowledge on the part of the audience to be published in more popular media. When you are prone to having fuzzy, slight ideas—as I am—a short lecture series published as a small book presents a wonderful opportunity to indulge your vice.

These particular lectures are what we might call a meditation inspired by some of the things that I have learned in the course of my main current research project, which is a reexamination of the long-neglected field of economic geography. I began that the way economists of my generation and temperament generally do: with a cute if grossly unrealistic model that seemed to me to yield some useful insights. Over the past several years I have been gradually elaborating on that original model, trying to make it increasingly realistic, trying to bring it into confrontation with data, trying to grasp at the deeper principles that one hopes underlie the special cases I have looked at so far. This is, of course, the way that academic economists work in the late twentieth century, and I am very much a part of my intellectual culture.

In the course of this work, however, I became increasingly and uncomfortably aware that the field in which I was working had a rather strange history. Economic geography—the location of activity in space—is a subject of obvious practical importance and presumably of considerable intellectual interest. Yet it is almost completely absent from the standard corpus of economic theory. My main objective over the past few years has been to remedy that omission the only way I know how: by producing clever, persuasive models that in turn help inspire students and colleagues to work on the subject. But I could not help becoming interested in understanding why my profession had ignored the questions I was now having so much fun answering.

I also became aware of a somewhat different but related history in another field, economic development, where a set of ideas similar to those that I was now applying to geography had flourished briefly in the 1940s and 1950s, then were all but forgotten.

Confronted by these strange turnings in the evolution of economic thought, I have found myself playing the role of an amateur intellectual historian, reading old and neglected papers, trying to make sense of the reasons why some ideas fail despite their seeming plausibility. And at the same time I found myself trying to justify the way in which I and my friends do research—even though the limiting nature of our intellectual style was made all too obvious by my dabblings in intellectual history.

Here, then, are some meditations on the nature of economic theory. I hope that some readers will find them enlightening, and that the rest will at least find them entertaining.

1   The Fall and Rise of Development Economics

A friend of mine who combines a professional interest in Africa with a hobby of collecting antique maps has written a fascinating paper on what he calls "the evolution of ignorance" about Africa. The paper describes how European maps of the African continent evolved from the fifteenth to the nineteenth centuries.[1]

You might have supposed that the process would have been more or less linear: as European knowledge of the continent advanced, the maps would have shown both increasing accuracy and increasing levels of detail. But that's not what happened. In the fifteenth century, maps of Africa were, of course, quite inaccurate about distances, coastlines, and so on. They did, however, contain quite a lot of information about the interior, based essentially on second- or third-hand travelers' reports. Thus the maps showed Timbuktu, the River Niger, and so forth. Admittedly, they also contained quite a lot of untrue information, like regions inhabited by men with their mouths in their stomachs. Still, in the early fifteenth century Africa on maps was a filled space.

Over time, the art of mapmaking and the quality of information used to make maps got steadily better. The coastline of Africa was first explored, then plotted with growing accuracy, and by the eighteenth century that coastline was shown in a manner essentially indistinguishable from that of modern maps. Cities and peoples along the coast were also shown with great fidelity.

On the other hand, the interior emptied out. The weird mythical creatures were gone, but so were the real cities and rivers. In a way, Europeans had become more ignorant about Africa than they had been before.

It should be obvious what happened: the improvement in the art of mapmaking raised the standard for what was considered valid data. Second-hand reports of the form "six days south of the end of the desert you encounter a vast river flowing from east to west" were no longer something you would use to draw your map. Only features of the landscape that had been visited by reliable informants equipped with sextants and compasses now qualified. And so the crowded if confused continental interior of the old maps became "darkest Africa," an empty space.

Of course, by the end of the nineteenth century darkest Africa had been explored, and mapped accurately. In the end, the rigor of modern cartography led to much better maps. But there was an extended period in which improved technique actually led to some loss in knowledge.

Now don't get worried—although I have put the word "geography" into the title of these lectures, they won't be about mapmaking, or at least not about the kind of map that can be placed on a wall. What I will be talking about is the evolution of ideas in economics—specifically, with the story of the two related disciplines of development economics and economic geography.

Of course doing economics, or for that matter just about any kind of intellectual inquiry, is a kind of mapmaking.

The economic theorist is in possession of information about the economy—some of it hard data, the equivalent of the work of men with sextants, some of it anecdotal, the equivalent of travelers' tales. From this mixture of reliable and unreliable evidence, plus a priori beliefs that are used not only to fill in where evidence is lacking but also in some cases to overrule the apparent evidence, the theorist attempts to put together a picture of how the economy works.

But how complete is that picture? In these lectures I will present an interpretation of the evolution of ideas in the two fields of development and economic geography. I will argue that in each of these fields, between the 1940s and the 1970s, there was a cycle somewhat similar to the story of how improved mapmaking temporarily diminished European knowledge about Africa. A rise in the standards of rigor and logic led to a much improved level of understanding of some things, but for a time it also led to an unwillingness to confront those areas that the new technical rigor could not yet reach. Areas of inquiry that had been filled in, however imperfectly, became blanks. Only gradually, over an extended period, did these dark regions get reexplored.

Why do I select these two fields? First, because of a common intellectual basis. Both development economics and economic geography experienced a flowering after World War II, resting on the same basic insight: the division of labor is limited by the extent of the market, but the extent of the market is in turn affected by the division of labor. The circularity of this relationship means that countries may experience self-reinforcing industrialization (or failure to industrialize), and that regions may experience self-reinforcing agglomeration.

What links development and geography is, however, not merely the common set of ideas that helped motivate them at one point in their history, but the specific problem that, I will argue, led to the failure of that set of ideas to become part of mainstream economic thinking.

Why do economists reject ideas? To laymen the unwillingness of academic economists to take seriously ideas that seem to them perfectly reasonable, whether they are John Kenneth Galbraith's theory of the new industrial state or George Gilder's views about wealth and poverty, is often infuriating. They can't understand the criteria; why isn't one forcefully written argument, backed by anecdotal evidence and an appeal to history, as good as another? And it is not at all uncommon for frustrated people with strong views about economics to attribute the unwillingness of the academic mainstream to listen to them or their friends to base motives—to a guild mentality that refuses to consider ideas that are not from the right people or expressed in the right jargon—or to political bias.

But the truth is less simple. Economists, like everyone, have their political biases, but these are by no means as strong an influence on what they are willing to consider as you might think. For example, one might have thought that strongly liberal economists like, say, James Tobin would be at least mildly sympathetic to the views of radical economists who draw their inspiration from Marx, or of heterodox economic thinkers like Galbraith. After all, in such fields as history and sociology the Marxist or post-Marxist left has long received a respectful hearing. And yet you don't find this happening: liberal economists are almost as quick as their conservative colleagues to condemn heterodox leftist ideas as foolish—it was the liberal Robert

Solow, not Milton Friedman, who defended orthodoxy in the bitter "capital controversy" with British radicals.

Similarly, one might have expected to find conservative economists willing to say nice things about their political allies in the supply-side camp, and perhaps to appoint a few supply-side true believers to their departments. But in fact they do not, even at fiercely conservative departments like those at Minnesota or Carnegie-Mellon.

So is it just guild mentality? Do you have to have a Ph.D. to be listened to? Well, having a Ph.D.—even having an established professional reputation—is no guarantee that your economic ideas will be treated with respect. Consider John Kenneth Galbraith or Lester Thurow, both leading economists in the view of the general public, both with all the formal qualifications, both totally ignored by the academic mainstream. Or consider Robert Mundell, who is still revered for his contributions to international monetary theory, yet whose later incarnation as the father of supply-side economics has similarly been ignored. And on the other hand, a nonacademic may under some conditions receive a respectful hearing—in the last few years Jane Jacobs, the maverick urban observer, has become something of a patron saint of the new growth theory.

So what is it that makes some ideas acceptable, while others are not? The answer—which is obvious to anyone immersed in economic research yet mysterious to outsiders—is that to be taken seriously an idea has to be *something you can model.* A properly modeled idea is, in modern economics, the moral equivalent of a properly surveyed region for eighteenth-century mapmakers.

For the moment, let me leave on one side the question of what constitutes a "proper" economic model—and how our notion of what is proper has changed over time. (I'll say more on the subject later in this lecture and elaborate further in the third lecture). But what seems clear to me is that the reason that the development theory that emerged in the 1940s and the economic geography that emerged more or less in parallel failed to "make it" into mainstream economics was the inability of their creators to express their ideas in a way suitable for the modeling techniques available at the time. In both development and geography the crucial problem, in particular, was the inability of the field's pioneers to be explicit about *market structure*—that is, about the conditions of competition in the hypothetical economies they were describing. It's a subtle problem; indeed, it is virtually impossible to explain why it is an issue at all to anyone who has not tried to engage in serious economic modeling. And yet the market structure issue proved fatal to efforts to integrate both development and geography into the mainstream of economic theory.

All this may sound fairly abstract. So let me turn to my first example: the story of the rise, fall, and resurrection of development economics.

Once upon a time there was a field called development economics—a branch of economics concerned with explaining why some countries are so much poorer than others, and with prescribing ways for poor countries to become rich. In the field's glory days in the 1950s the ideas of development economics were regarded as revolutionary and important, and commanded both great intellectual prestige and substantial real-world influence. Moreover, development economics attracted creative minds and was marked by a great deal of intellectual excitement.

That field no longer exists. There are, of course, many excellent people who work on the economics of developing countries. Some of the problems they address are essentially generic to all countries, but there are also issues that are characteristic of poorer countries in particular, and in this sense there is a field that focuses on the economics of underdevelopment. But it is a diffuse field: those who work on the economics of, say, Third World agriculture have little if any overlap with those who work on LDC trade in manufactures, and these in turn hardly talk to those who focus on the macroeconomics of debt and hyperinflation. And very few economists would now presume to offer grand hypotheses about why poor countries are poor, or what they can do about it. In effect, a counterrevolution swept away development economics.

And yet there is now a growing sense that this counterrevolution went too far. In the last few years it has become apparent that during the 1940s and 1950s, a core of ideas emerged regarding external economies, strategic complementarity, and economic development that remains intellectually valid and may continue to have practical applications. This set of ideas—which I will refer to as "high development theory"[2]—anticipated in a number of ways the cutting edge of modern trade and growth theory.

But these ideas have had to be rediscovered. Between 1960 and 1980 high development theory was virtually buried, essentially because the founders of development economics failed to make their points with sufficient analytical clarity to communicate their essence to other economists, and perhaps even to each other. Only recently have changes in economics made it possible to reconsider what the development theorists said, and to regain the valuable ideas that have been lost.

The Big Push

A good place to start our discussion is with the paper that really began the golden age of development economics: Paul Rosenstein-Rodan's "Problems of Industrialization of Eastern and South-Eastern Europe." It is a quite straightforward paper, yet it has inspired astonishingly many interpretations. Some economists read it as essentially Keynesian, a story about interactions between the multiplier and the accelerator. Rosenstein-Rodan himself seems to have had a more or less Keynesian idea about effective demand in mind, with (as we will see) considerable justification. Other economists saw it as an assertion that growth must be somehow "balanced" in order to be successful—indeed, Albert Hirschman cast his celebrated *The Strategy of Economic Development* as a refutation of Rosenstein-Rodan and others of the balanced growth school, which I will argue was both a misunderstanding and self-destructive. Yet other economists tried to generate low-level equilibrium traps by invoking such mechanisms as interactions among income, savings, and population growth (e.g., Leibenstein 1957, Nelson 1956); such mechanisms can also justify a Big Push, but they are very far from the spirit of the original story.

In the late 1980s, however, Murphy, Shleifer, and Vishny (1989) offered a formalization of the Big Push that is quite close to the original spirit, and that is also quite revealing about the essential aspects of high development theory. Let me offer a slightly streamlined presentation of their model, and then ask what it tells us.

Imagine, then, an economy that is closed to international trade. (This sounds archaic and way off the point in our current age of export-led economic miracles, and perhaps it is—although I'll argue later that we may be able to modify the story to make it relevant to modern economies. But in any case, for the moment let's play by the original rules.) Our hypothetical economy can be described by assumptions about factor supply, technology, demand, and market structure.

Factor Supply The economy is endowed with only a single factor of production—labor—in fixed total supply L. Labor can be employed in either of two sectors: a "traditional" sector, characterized by constant returns, or a "modern" sector, characterized by increasing returns. Although the same factor of production is used in the traditional and modern sectors, it is not paid the same wage. Labor must be paid a premium to move from traditional to modern employment. Let $w > 1$ be the ratio of the wage rate that must be paid in the modern sector to that in the traditional sector.

Technology It is assumed that the economy produces N goods, where N is a large number. We choose units so that the productivity of labor in the traditional sector is unity in each of the goods. In the modern sector, unit labor requirements are decreasing in the scale of production. For simplicity, decreasing costs take a linear form. Let Q_i be the production of good i in the modern sector. Then if the modern sector produces the good at all, the labor requirement will be assumed to take the form

$$L_i = F + cQ_i, \tag{1}$$

where $c < 1$ is the marginal labor requirement. Notice that for this example it is assumed that the relationship between input and output is the same for all N goods.

Demand   Demand for the N goods is Cobb-Douglas and symmetric. That is, each good receives a constant share $1/N$ of expenditure. The model will be static, with no asset accumulation or decumulation; so expenditure equals income.

Market Structure   The traditional sector is assumed to be characterized by perfect competition. Thus for each good there is a perfectly elastic supply from the traditional sector at the marginal cost of production; given our choice of units, this supply price is unity in terms of traditional sector labor. By contrast, a single entrepreneur is assumed to have the unique ability to produce each good in the modern sector.

How will such a producer price? Given the assumption of Cobb-Douglas demand and a large number of goods, she will face unit-elastic demand. If she were an unconstrained monopolist, she would therefore raise her price without limit. But potential competition from the traditional sector puts a limit on the price: she cannot go above a price of 1 (in terms of traditional labor) without being undercut by traditional producers. So each producer in the modern sector will set the same price, unity, as would have been charged in the traditional sector.

We can now ask the question, will production actually take place in the traditional or the modern sector? To answer this, we draw a simple diagram (figure 1.1). On the horizontal axis is the labor input, L_i, used to produce a typical good. On the vertical axis is that sector's output Q_i. The two solid lines represent the technologies of production in the two sectors: a 45-degree line for the traditional sector, a line with a slope of $1/c$ for the modern sector.

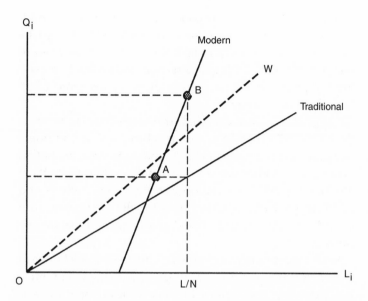

Figure 1.1

From this figure it is immediately possible to read off what the economy would produce if all labor were allocated either to the modern or the traditional sector. In either case L/N workers would be employed in the production of each good. If all goods are produced traditionally, each good would have an output Q^1. If they are all produced using modern techniques, the output is Q^2. As drawn, $Q^2 > Q^1$; this will be the case provided that

$$\frac{(L/N) - F}{c} > L/N,$$ (2)

that is, as long as the marginal cost advantage of modern production is sufficiently large and/or fixed costs are not too large. Since this is the interesting case, we focus on it.

But even if the economy could produce more using modern methods, this does not mean that it will. It must be profitable for each individual entrepreneur in the modern sector to produce, taking into account the necessity of paying the premium wage w—as well as the decisions of all the other entrepreneurs.

Suppose that an individual firm starts modern production while all other goods are produced using traditional techniques. The firm will charge the same price as that on other goods and hence sell the same amount; since there are many goods, we may neglect any income effects and suppose that each good continues to sell Q^1. Thus this firm would have the production and employment illustrated by point A.

Is this a profitable move? The firm uses less labor than would be required for traditional production, but must pay that labor more. Draw in a ray from the origin whose slope is the modern relative wage w; OW in the figure is an example. Then modern production is profitable given traditional production elsewhere if and only if OW passes *below* A. As I've drawn it here, this test is of course failed: it is not profitable for an individual firm to start modern production.

On the other hand, suppose that all modern firms start simultaneously. Then each firm will produce Q^2, leading to production and employment at point B. Again, this will be profitable if the wage line OW passes below B. As drawn, this test *is* satisfied.

Obviously, there are three possible outcomes.[3] If the wage premium $w - 1$ is low, the economy always "industrializes"; if it is high, it never industrializes; and if it takes on an intermediate value, there are both low- and high-level equilibria.

One would hardly conclude from this model that the existence of multiple equilibria is highly likely, even given the assumptions that such multiple equilibria will occur only for some parameter values. And it is easy to critique the plausibility of the assumptions. Yet the model can serve as a useful jumping-off point for thinking about development models.

Some Analytical Implications

The Big Push model may be viewed as a minimalist demonstration of the potential role of pecuniary external economies for development; of the necessary conditions for such external economies; and of what a model of external economies must include.

External Economies   It is clear that when there are two equilibria in this model the movement from one to the other involves meaningful external economies. This is true even if one takes the wage premium for the modern sector to represent payment for the disutility of modern life, that is, regards the gain in wages when workers move from traditional to modern jobs as having no welfare significance. Even in that case, the industrialized equilibrium leaves workers indifferent while generating profits that would otherwise not exist. If one instead offers some kind of efficiency-wage or surplus labor argument that places at least partial value on the rise in wages, the case is that much stronger.

But there are no technological external economies in the model. Why do pecuniary external economies matter here?

Necessary Conditions   Two conditions are necessary to generate external economies in this model. First, there must be economies of scale in production. This is obvious from the geometry: if there were no fixed costs in the modern sector, the profitability of modern firms would not depend on how many other firms were using modern techniques.

Second, the modern sector must be able to draw labor out of a traditional sector that pays lower wages. I would like to stretch the point a bit here and think of the essence of the condition as being that there is an elastic supply of labor to the modern sector, labor that would not be employed in equally productive occupations otherwise. (This is what gives the model its vaguely Keynesian feel.) So it is the *interaction* between *internal* economies of scale and elastic factor supplies that gives rise to de facto *external* economies.

Modeling A final point, which is crucial. To write a coherent model of the Big Push, it is necessary somehow to deal with the problem of market structure. As long as there are unexhausted economies of scale in the modern sector, which are crucial to the whole argument, one must face up to the necessity of modeling the modern sector as imperfectly competitive. In the Murphy et al. formulation, imperfect competition is dealt with by assuming a set of limit-pricing monopolists. This works well here, although (as we will see) it is not always an adequate device. The point is, however, that one must deal with the issue somehow. To the extent that there is anything to high development theory, it is intimately bound up with imperfect competition. If one tries to fudge that issue, as many economists have, one ends up with mush.

Unfortunately, there are no general or even plausible tractable models of imperfect competition. The tractable models always involve some set of arbitrary assumptions about tastes, technology, behavior, or all three. This means that to do development theory, one must have the courage to be silly, writing down models that are implausible in the details in order to arrive at convincing higher-level insights.

This is not a new lesson. Trade theorists learned it more than a dozen years ago, when they realized that a reconstruction of trade theory to take account of increasing returns would necessarily involve abandoning all pretense of generality; growth theorists learned the same lesson a few years later. High development theory faltered because it did not take the same leap.

The Elements of High Development Theory

In the last section I presented a modern version of the Big Push model as a motivating and clarifying example. Now I want to turn back to the older development literature to extract a broader set of key elements.

Economies of Scale and External Economies

A casual reading of the development literature suggests that there is a dividing line circa 1960. Before 1960 writers on development generally assumed as a matter of course that economies of scale were a limiting factor on the ability to profitably establish industries in less developed countries, and that in the presence of such economies of scale pecuniary external economies assume real welfare significance. They seem, however, to have been unaware of the degree to which economies of scale raise problems for explicit modeling of competition, and/or of the extent to which the drive for formalism was pushing economics toward explicit models.

After 1960, by contrast, economists working on development had been trained in the formalism of constant-returns general equilibrium, and did not so much reject the possibility that economies of scale might matter as simply fail to notice it.

The Big Push model presented above is one in which economies of scale at the plant level, and an elastic supply of factors of production, interact to yield pecuniary external economies with real welfare significance. In retrospect, it is remarkable how clearly similar stories were presented in many papers from the era of high development theory—and also how unaware many of the authors seem to have been of the extent to which their conclusions depended crucially on the non-neoclassical assumption of significant unexploited scale economies.

We may begin with Rosenstein-Rodan (1943). In his seminal paper, he illustrated his argument for coordinated investment by imagining a country in which 20,000 (!) "unemployed workers ... are taken from the land and put into a large new shoe factory. They receive wages substantially higher than their previous income *in natura*." Rosenstein-Rodan then goes on to argue that this investment is likely to be unprofitable in isolation, but profitable if accompanied by similar investments in many other industries. Both key assumptions are clearly present: the assumption of economies of scale, embodied in the assertion that the factory must be established at such a large scale, and the assumption that these workers can be drawn elastically from unemployment or low-paying agricultural employment.

Some though not all subsequent development writers invoked economies of scale as key to external economies. In the best papers the basic story comes through very clearly. Fleming (1954) presented an analysis of the nature of external economies in development that focuses very clearly on the interaction between factor supply and scale economies—and that also, unlike Rosenstein-Rodan, points out clearly that the case for coordination falls apart without both assumptions.

Hirschman (1958) is not usually thought of as a thinker preoccupied with nonconvexities. Yet his explanation of the concept of backward linkages explicitly invokes the importance of achieving minimum economic scale, while his discussion of forward linkages more vaguely alludes to the role of scale as well.

So I would argue that high development theory circa 1958 did have as one of its central concepts the idea that economies of the scale at the level of the individual plant translated into increasing returns at the aggregate level via pecuniary external economies.

Admittedly, some of the literature of the time does not seem to agree with my argument that scale economies were a key element of the theory. Nurkse (1952), while accepting that indivisibilities play a role in virtuous circles of development, denies that they are essential. Scitovsky (1954), in making the clear distinction between technological and pecuniary external economies, makes the now classic point that in competitive equilibrium it is actually efficient to ignore pecuniary external effects. When he then searches for reasons to soften this conclusion, he provides only a single paragraph on scale effects, then turns to an extended discussion of expectational errors. Lewis's (1955) text on economic growth seems fairly innocent of the whole idea of external economies; indeed, the term does not even appear in the index. And Myrdal's (1957) exposition of the role of "circular and cumulative causation" sounds as if it must surely include a key role for economies of scale; but I have been unable to find a single reference to their role—even an indirect one—in his work. Indeed, when he offers an example of the process of circular causation, the external economies occur via the tax rate rather than any private market spillover.

So it may be giving too much credit to our intellectual forerunners to think of 1950s development theory as involving a general appreciation of the way in which economies of scale at the individual plant level can aggregate to strategic complementarity at the economy level. But at least some theorists seem to have understood the point quite clearly.

Factor Supply

Probably the most famous paper in all of development economics is Arthur Lewis's "Economic Development with Unlimited Supplies of Labor" (1954). In retrospect, it is hard to see exactly why. One interpretation of Lewis's argument is that the shadow price of labor drawn from the agricultural sector in developing countries is zero or at least low, so that the social return to investment in industry exceeds its private return. It was pretty obvious even early on, however, that this was a fragile basis on which to justify protection and promotion of industry.

Why then was Lewis so influential? The key reason, I would argue, was that the surplus labor story, unlike many other development stories emerging at the time, could be formalized relatively easily; so it gave economists a way to follow the mainstream's increasing emphasis on rigor and formalism while continuing to do development. But it was also true that even though Lewis himself made no reference to the external economy/development literature, his defense of the surplus labor idea helped shore up one of the key ideas of that literature. I've already pointed out that the assumption that additional labor in the manufacturing sector could come out of rural underemployment was central to Rosenstein-Rodan (1943). A few years later Fleming (1954) realized that in the absence of such an assumption industrial investments would be substitutes instead of complements.

Rosenstein-Rodan and Lewis stressed the elasticity of labor supply as a key factor in development. Other authors, such as Nurkse (1952), stressed the elasticity of capital supply. In particular, Hirschman (1958) emphasized at length the extent to which investment opportunities could bring forth additional savings. Again it may be stretching the point, but many development theorists in the 1950s seem to have been aware that elasticity of factor supply was also crucial to an external economy story of development.

Let me preview the next lecture a bit by pointing out that in regional economics and economic geography, it is entirely natural to assume high elasticity of factor supply *to a particular region*, since factors of production may be attracted from other regions. This is one reason why the tradition of high development theory remained alive much longer among geographers than among economists; development-type stories such as those of Pred (1966) continued to seem natural and plausible.

Backward and Forward Linkages

The idea of linkages is one of the greatest sources of confusion in thinking about both the theory of development

and development in practice. Hirschman (1958) introduced the term and presented it as something quite new.
Later commentators have taken him at his word. Thus
Little (1982) insists that since other authors had already
explored at some length (if with some confusion) the possible role of pecuniary external economies, Hirschman's
linkage concept must have crucially involved a nonpecu-
niary element. Yet in Hirschman's definition of backward
linkages, as already mentioned, the role of pecuniary externalities linked to economies of scale is quite explicit: an
industry creates a backward linkage when its demand en-
ables an upstream industry to be established at at least
minimum economic scale. The strength of an industry's
backward linkages is to be measured by the probability
that it will in fact push other industries over the threshold
of profitability.

Forward linkages are also defined by Hirschman as involving an interaction between scale and market size; in
this case the definition is vaguer, but seems to involve the
ability of an industry to reduce the costs of potential downstream users of its products and thus, again, push them
over the threshold.

Seen in this way, the concepts of forward and backward
linkages seem quite straightforward—and also less distinctive to Hirschman than is usually portrayed. Fleming
(1954), in particular, argued that the "horizontal" external
economies of Rosenstein-Rodan were less important than
the "vertical" external economies that result when intermediate goods are produced subject to scale economies,
which sounds awfully close to linkage theory.

It is also possible to offer simple formal models illustrat-
ing the concepts of forward and backward linkages. In-

deed, the Murphy et al. Big Push model can be seen as essentially driven by the backward linkages among goods, in which each good produced in the modern sector enlarges the markets for all other goods.

Forward linkages are a little harder to model. They ordinarily arise in the context of industries producing intermediate goods (although not always, as described below); this means that a more complex structure than the Murphy, Shleifer, Vishny version of the Big Push is necessary. Also, the limit-pricing assumption that makes imperfect competition easy in the Big Push model immediately rules out any forward linkage, since cost savings are never passed on to downstream consumers.

There are, however, slightly harder models in which both forward and backward linkages do appear. In particular, they pop up as obvious concepts in the models of economic geography I'll talk about in the next lecture.

As in the case of Lewis, it is slightly puzzling that Hirschman's work had such an impact. What he seems to have offered by way of distinct analysis were some hints about development planning. First, the focus on linkages involving intermediate goods rather than final demand suggested that development efforts could focus on a few strategic industries rather than seek an economywide Big Push—hence Hirschman's view that he was an opponent of Rosenstein-Rodan and Nurkse, even though they were far closer to one another in worldview than any of them was to the emerging views of mainstream economics. Second, Hirschman's discussion seemed to suggest that appropriate key industries could be identified by examining input-output tables—an exciting suggestion for the quantitatively oriented planner.

In fact, the concept of linkages, even as Hirschman presented it, implied no such thing. Let's think, for example, about backward linkages. What gives rise to an economically significant backward linkage in Hirschman's sense is not simply the fact that sector A buys the output of sector B; it is the assertion that investment in A, by increasing the size of B's market, induces a shift to more efficient large-scale production (or the substitution of domestic production for imports). Now one cannot infer this merely by observing a large entry in the AB cell of the input-output table—maybe B is already at efficient scale, or maybe even this expansion will not get it close to that scale. Nor can one even make a probabilistic argument that industries with any particular pattern of input purchases are especially likely to generate linkage effects. Which is better—an industry that buys from only a few other sectors, and is therefore more likely to bring any one of them to critical mass, or an industry that buys a little from many sectors, and therefore has more chances to push one of them over the top?

Indeed, if you try to use the rhetoric of linkages without understanding that it is an argument that depends crucially on economies of scale, you end up speaking nonsense. I once saw an industrial policy advocate argue that we should promote industries that buy from or sell to many other sectors. I wonder which industries he thought he could exclude from that definition—hand-thrown pottery?

In general, it seems best to regard "linkages" as simply a particularly evocative phrase for the strategic complementarities that arise when individual goods are produced subject to economies of scale. This in effect argues that

Hirschman's distinctive contribution was more one of style than of substance, a point to which I will return below.

Summary

In this part of the lecture I have argued that a number of works in development economics written during the 1950s contained, more or less explicitly and more or less self-consciously, a theory in which strategic complementarity played a key role in development: external economies arose from a circular relationship in which the decision to invest in large-scale production depended on the size of the market, and the size of the market depended on the decision to invest. Whatever the practical relevance of this theory, it made perfectly good logical sense.

Yet this development theory was subsequently abandoned, to such an extent that classic papers in the field began to seem, as the physicist Wolfgang Pauli used to say, "not even wrong"—simply incomprehensible. We next turn to the reasons for that decline and abandonment.

The Failure of High Development Theory

Why did development economics fade away? One can, with some justification, offer the cynical explanation that the field waned with its funding. After all, development economists were most often consulted or given positions of influence in connection with the disbursement of foreign aid. As foreign aid became increasingly unpopular with the electorates of rich nations, and as the real value of such aid not only failed to keep pace with gross world product but actually declined, development economics became a much less exciting career. One may also argue that development economics was discredited by lack of practical success. After all, relative to the hopes of the 1950s and even the 1960s, the performance of most developing countries has been dismal. (Indeed, the polite phrase "developing country" itself has become an embarrassment, when it must be used in such sentences as "Per capita income in the developing countries of Sub-Saharan Africa has declined steadily since the mid-1970s.") It is unfair to blame Western economists for more than a small fraction of this failure, but the ideas of development economics were too often used as a justification for policies that in retrospect impeded growth rather than helping it along. Where rapid economic growth did occur, it occurred in ways that were not anticipated by the development theorists.

Yet neither declining external demand for development economists nor their practical failures fully explain the sputtering out of the field. Purely intellectual problems were also extremely important. In particular, during the years when high development theory flourished, the leading development economists failed to turn their intuitive insights into clear-cut models that could serve as the core of an enduring discipline.

From the point of view of a modern economist, the most striking feature of the works of high development theory is their adherence to a discursive, nonmathematical style. Economics has, of course, become vastly more mathematical over time. Nonetheless, development economics was archaic in style even for its own time. Of the four most famous high development works, Rosenstein-Rodan's was approximately contemporary with Samuelson's formulation of the Heckscher-Ohlin model, while Lewis, Myrdal, and Hirschman were all roughly contemporary with Solow's initial statement of growth theory.

This lack of formality was not because development economists were peculiarly mathematically incapable. Hirschman made a significant contribution to the formal theory of devaluation in the 1940s, while Fleming helped create the still influential Mundell-Fleming model of floating exchange rates. Moreover, the development field itself was at the same time generating mathematical planning models—first Harrod-Domar type growth models, then linear programming approaches—that were actually quite technically advanced for their time.

So why didn't high development theory get expressed in formal models? Almost certainly for one basic reason: the difficulty of reconciling economies of scale with a competitive market structure.

The example of the Big Push model discussed earlier in this lecture shows that models in the spirit of high development theory need not be very complicated. They must, however, deal somehow with the problem of market structure. This essentially means making some peculiar assumptions that allow one to exploit the bag of tricks that industrial organization theorists developed for thinking about such issues in the 1970s. In the 1950s, although the technical level of development economists was actually quite high enough to have allowed them to do the same thing, the bag of tricks wasn't there. So development theorists were placed in an awkward bind, with basically sensible ideas that they could not quite express in fully worked-out models. And the drift of the economics profession made the situation worse. In the 1940s and even in the 1950s, it was still possible for an economist to publish a paper that made persuasive points verbally, without tying up all the loose ends. After 1960, however, an attempt to publish a paper like Rosenstein-Rodan's would have immediately gotten a grilling: "Why not build a smaller factory (for which the market is adequate)? Oh, you're assuming economies of scale? But that means imperfect competition, and nobody knows how to model that, so this paper doesn't make any sense." It seems safe to say that such a paper would have been unpublishable any time after 1970, if not earlier.

Some development theorists responded by getting as close to a formal model as they could. This is to some extent true of Rosenstein-Rodan, and certainly the case for Fleming (1954), which gets painfully close to being a full model. But others at least professed to see a less formal, less disciplined approach as a virtue. It is in this light that one needs to see Hirschman and Myrdal. These authors are often cited today (by me among others) as forerunners of the recent emphasis in several fields on strategic complementarity. In fact, however, their books marked the end, not the beginning, of high development theory. Myrdal's central thesis was the idea of "circular causation." But the idea of circular causation is essentially already there in Allyn Young (1928), not to mention Rosenstein-Rodan; and Nurkse in 1952 referred repeatedly to the circular nature of the problem of getting growth going in poor countries. So Myrdal was in effect providing a capsulization of an already extensive and familiar set of ideas rather than a new departure. Similarly, Hirschman's idea of linkages was more distinctive for the effectiveness of the term and the policy advice that he derived loosely from it than for its intellectual novelty; in effect Rosenstein-Rodan was already talking about linkages, and Fleming very explicitly had both forward and backward linkages in his discussion.

What marked Myrdal and Hirschman was not so much the novelty of their ideas but their stylistic and methodological stance. Until their books, economists doing high development theory were trying to be good mainstream economists. They could not develop full formal models, but they got as close as they could, trying to keep close to the increasingly model-oriented mainstream. Myrdal and Hirschman abandoned this effort, and eventually in effect took stands on principle against any effort to formalize their ideas.

One imagines that this was initially very liberating for them and their followers. Yet in the end it was a vain stance. Economic theory is essentially a collection of models. Broad insights that are not expressed in model form may temporarily attract attention and even win converts, but they do not endure unless codified in a reproducible— and teachable—form. You may not like this tendency; certainly economists tend to be too quick to dismiss what has not been formalized (although I believe that the focus on models is basically right). Like it or not, however, the influence of ideas that have not been embalmed in models soon decays. And this was the fate of high development theory. Myrdal's effective presentation of the idea of circular and cumulative causation, or Hirschman's evocation of linkages, were stimulating and immensely influential in the 1950s and early 1960s. By the 1970s (when I was a student of economics), they had come to seem not so much wrong as meaningless. What were these guys talking about? Where were the models? And so high development theory was not so much rejected as simply bypassed.

The exception proves the rule. Lewis's surplus labor concept was the model that launched a thousand papers; even though surplus labor assumptions were already standard among development theorists, the empirical basis for assuming surplus labor was weak, and the idea of external economies/strategic complementarity was surely more interesting. The point was, of course, that precisely because he did not mix economies of scale into his framework, Lewis offered theorists something they could model using available tools.

But surplus labor was too thin an idea on which to base an enduring field. To be sure, for a while dual-economy models—with constant returns and perfect competition—were a staple of development courses. With the key role of dualism in justifying the Big Push lost, however, these dual-economy models gradually came to seem pointless. By 1980 or so, virtually all vestiges of high development theory had disappeared from development economics. In that sense, the whole enterprise of high development theory was a failure.

The irony, of course, is that high development theory was right. By this I do not mean that the Big Push is really the right story of how development takes place, or even that the issues raised in high development theory are necessarily the key ones for making poor countries rich. What I do mean is that the unconventional themes put forth by the high development theorists—their emphasis on strategic complementarity in investment decisions and on the problem of coordination failure—did in fact identify important possibilities that are neglected in competitive equilibrium models. But the high development theorists failed to convince their colleagues of the importance of those possibilities. Worse, they failed even to communicate clearly what they were talking about. And so good ideas, important ideas, were ignored for a generation after they were first enunciated.

Was the failure in the high development theorists, or the economics profession, or both? Or was it nobody's fault, but simply a preordained path that could not have been avoided? I'm not ready to answer these questions yet. First, I want to take a look at a largely parallel story that nonetheless lets us see things from a somewhat different perspective: the failure of economics to take account of space.

2 Geography Lost and Found

Anyone who owns an atlas has noticed at some point that the Brazilian bulge of South America seems to fit almost exactly into the facing indentation on the coast of Africa. At least a few people have long been aware that if you make cutouts of the outlines of the continents and treat the assemblage as a kind of jigsaw puzzle, the pieces fit together passably well into a single giant land mass—and the fit is considerably improved if you include the continental shelves as well as the dry land. But until the middle of the 1960s this observation was pretty much ignored by geologists. A heretic like Alfred Wegener might claim that the fit was too good to be coincidence, that it demonstrated that continents were somehow drifting pieces of a primordial supercontinent. But mainstream geology could conceive of no mechanism for such drift, and thus ignored his ideas.

So how did mainstream geology account for the shapes of the continents? Indeed, how did it account for the existence of the continents, or for that matter of all of the aspects of the earth's surface that we now believe to be the result of plate tectonics—such as fault lines, rings of volcanoes, and for that matter mountain ranges? The answer, by and large, is that mainstream geology simply put those questions to one side. It was clear that mountain ranges were lifted by *something;* that something was labeled "earth forces," presumably driven somehow by the planet's internal heat, and otherwise left unexplained. Instead, geologists focused on what they did understand, which meant primarily the forces that tear mountains down—erosion, glacial action, etc.—rather than those that build them up.

Of course, all that changed with the discovery of seafloor spreading in the 1960s. Suddenly there was a mechanism for continental drift—and as soon as that mechanism made the concept intellectually respectable, a whole new set of facts became relevant. Does Brazil seem to fit neatly into the Bight of Benin? Do the Alps look like land buckled by an Italian peninsula that has smashed into the European mainland, or the Himalayas like the result of India doing the same to Asia? All of these previously useless observations suddenly made sense and became obvious confirmations of the new view.

There are clearly parallels between the story of how geologists ignored the shapes of continents and the locations of mountain ranges and the story of how European mapmakers threw out the informal knowledge their predecessors had about Africa's interior. In some ways, however, the story is even starker. For one thing, the importance of the ability to model stands out even more clearly in this case: continental drift was an unacceptable, indeed almost incomprehensible, hypothesis because geologists could not think of how to model such a process. And the response of the geological profession was a remarkable, although typical one: virtually to ignore, even to deny the existence of, questions that it was not prepared to answer.

In the previous lecture I described the history of thought in development economics as being like the history of European mapping of Africa: the rich if unreliable insights of the early explorers, the development theorists of the 1940s and 1950s, were eventually ruled inadmissible as evidence because those insights could not be clearly modeled. Still, nobody forgot that the continent had an interior; development economics as a subject remained an acknowledged area of importance, even if much of its distinctive content got lost.

The history of economic geography—of the study of the location of economic activity—is more like the story of geological thought about the shapes and location of continents and mountain ranges. The location of production is an obvious feature of the economic world. Indeed, I began to get interested in economics as a schoolchild by looking at those old-fashioned maps of countries that used picturesque symbols to represent economic activity: sheaves of wheat to represent agriculture, little miners' carts to represent resource extraction, little factories to represent industry, and so on. And yet there is almost no spatial analysis in mainstream economics. It is almost forty years since Walter Isard attacked economic analysis for taking place in a "wonderland of no spatial dimensions," yet his plea for spatial economics has gone virtually unanswered.

Consider, for example, the latest entrant in the field of economic principles textbooks: Joseph Stiglitz's *Economics*. It's a widely acclaimed book, faulted if at all for its excessive comprehensiveness, which accounts for its 1,100-plus page length. Yet the index contains no reference to the words "location" or "spatial economics," and has precisely one reference to "cities"—which occurs in the course of a discussion of rural-urban migration in less developed countries.

Why this neglect? Mark Blaug, in his magisterial survey of economic thought, describes the neglect of spatial issues as a "major puzzle," which in the end he explains by historical happenstance: because von Thünen was German, the tradition of spatial analysis failed to get established in the eventually dominant Anglo-Saxon school. But this is too easy an answer. On one side, it fails to appreciate the sociology of late twentieth-century economic research: in the world I inhabit, populated by hundreds if not thousands of technically able researchers desperate for interesting questions to study, any obviously available intellectual territory will always be exploited.[1] Even though there is surely an excessive bias toward cultivating the internal margin, finding new theoretical wrinkles on familiar topics or using heavy econometric artillery to tease a bit more out of well-studied data, it is highly implausible that a huge extensive margin like the economics of location would be neglected simply because it failed to get into the curriculum a century ago.

Moreover, although Ricardo and Mill may have neglected the economics of space, there has been no lack of influential later efforts to persuade the profession to put location on the intellectual map. In particular, Walter Isard made a powerful effort to get his fellow economists to take space seriously, an effort that among other things involved digesting the German tradition in location and making it accessible both in language and in style to the world of English-speaking economists. And in the late 1960s and early 1970s there was a significant boomlet in the "new urban economics," a subject whose models derived directly from von Thünen's *Isolated State*.

So why did spatial issues remain a blind spot for the economic profession? It was not a historical accident: there was something about spatial economics that made it inherently unfriendly terrain for the kind of modeling mainstream economists know how to do.

That something was, as you might well guess, the problem of market structure in the face of increasing returns, a problem that is even more acute in economic geography than in development economics. In development the crucial role that high development theory assigned to increasing returns was a hypothesis crucial to that doctrine, but not necessarily crucial to understanding development in general. One could do meaningful theorizing about developing countries, albeit not in the grand tradition, without sacrificing the convenient assumptions of constant returns and perfect competition. In spatial economics, however, you really cannot get started at all without finding a way to deal with scale economies and oligopolistic firms.

The reason has been well understood by many if not all urban and spatial economists, and is sometimes referred to as the problem of "backyard capitalism." The parable goes something like this: imagine (as spatial theorists often do) that the world consists of a homogeneous, featureless plain; imagine further that there are transportation costs; and finally suppose for a moment that there are *no* economies of scale. Would such a world give rise to the highly uneven spatial distribution of economic activity we actually see, in which most people live on the small urbanized fraction of the land, and in which urban areas themselves are highly specialized? (This paragraph was written after a disheartening look at real estate prices in Palo Alto—that is, in the crowded heart of Silicon Valley.) The answer, of course, is that it would not. The efficient thing (and also the market outcome, since this would be an undistorted, Pareto-efficient world) would be to have production of every commodity spread evenly across the plain, so that no transportation is necessary. In the literal absence of any scale economies we would not even see a world of small villages—we would see one of self-sufficient family farms.

Now it is true that the real world isn't a homogeneous plain. Those sheaves of wheat and little mining carts on my childhood maps tell us as much. Yet few would argue that natural resources explain more than a fraction of the observed unevenness of economic activity across space—what exactly is the resource that explains why 11 million people are in Greater Los Angeles, or 17 million in São Paulo? And indeed even the distribution of agricultural production is dictated as much by access to urban markets as by the underlying quality of the soil—a point made by von Thünen at the very beginning of location theory.

No, in order to talk even halfway sensibly about economic geography it is necessary to invoke the role of increasing returns in some form. And that means that even to get started on the subject one must get into the issues that, as I argued in the last lecture, did so much to make high development theory unacceptable to mainstream economics.

And so how did the mainstream cope with spatial issues? By ignoring them. Never mind that the importance of location confronts us continually in daily life, or for that matter that urban systems exhibit empirical regularities as strong as any in economics. Like geologists who could not really look at where mountain ranges are located because they knew they had no model of mountain formation, economists avoided looking at the spatial aspect of economies because they knew they had no way to model that aspect.

This may seem like a strong statement to make in isolation. So let me now turn to a brief survey of what seem to me, with the benefit of hindsight, to have been the most important traditions in spatial economics before, say, 1980. I hope that by the end of this discussion I will have persuaded you that my diagnosis is basically right.

Five Traditions in Economic Geography

These lectures are a meditation on economic theory, not a scholarly history of thought. As a consequence, I take the liberty of being both casual and dictatorial about my attributions. I will not worry too much about who exactly had priority in some idea; thus while Mark Blaug, in his *Economic Theory in Retrospect*, tells us that Launhardt not only was the real author of much that we attribute to von Thünen but also anticipated much of Weber, I will refer to Weber and von Thünen, since those are the "brand names" under which certain ideas have come to be known. I will also give short shrift to a vast literature, partly because I am not anywhere near as well read in it as I would like to be, partly because I want to make a point rather than survey a field.

In other words, I want to do for spatial economics the same thing I did for development economics in the last lecture: use a biased set of references to argue that there was a set of core ideas that make considerable sense in light of recent economic analysis, but that were unacceptable to mainstream economics because they could not at that time be modeled.

The task is, however, a bit harder this time, because the tradition in spatial economics is both longer and more diffuse than that in development. In fact, my personal classification system identifies not one but five traditions in the field. Of these five, I will argue that four are really different ways of looking at the same thing—although their proponents did not see it that way, and indeed tended to view them as rival alternatives. The fifth, the tradition of land rent/land use analysis going back to von Thünen himself, is the orphan, largely divorced conceptually from the other approaches. Not coincidentally, it is also the tradition that has been most readily embraced by mainstream economics.

So let me begin my survey, with the first and, to my mind, least appealing of these traditions.

Germanic Geometry

When one mentions "location theory" to most economists, they think (if they think of anything) of the tradition that flourished in Germany in the first half of this century, a tradition concerned with a distinctive problem: the geometry of location on a two-dimensional landscape.

It is usual to divide this tradition into two subsets. First came Alfred Weber and his followers, who analyzed the location decision of a firm serving one or more markets and relying on one or more sources of supply, with the total number of such relevant points not less than three. (Otherwise the firm would always choose to locate on top of either the input source or the market.) Then came the tradition of central-place theory, which analyzed the location and roles of manufacturing/marketing/etc. centers serving a hypothetical evenly spread agricultural population. In this tradition, Lösch had the big geometric insight—that

market areas should be hexagonal—while Christaller produced the empirically fruitful idea that there should be a
hierarchy of central places, with nested market areas.

Both Weberian location theory and central-place theory
have been subjected to many critiques over the years,
many of them focusing on the unrealism of the assumptions about the distribution of demand, the relationship between transport costs and distance, and so on. I don't think
that charges of unrealism are to the point: when you are
working in a very new area, it is entirely forgivable to
make outrageous simplifications in pursuit of insights,
with the faith that the model can be brought closer to the
facts on later passes. (This is a self-serving remark, and
also a preview of the third lecture.) And in any case
this kind of criticism was surely not the reason why the
Germanic tradition failed to make it into mainstream
economics—after all, one could hardly accuse J. R. Hicks,
whose *Value and Capital* was roughly contemporary with
the development of central-place theory, of robust realism.

Rather, the problem with the German tradition must
surely have been that it seemed to be about geometry, not
about economics as the increasingly dominant Anglo-
Saxon mainstream understood it. That is, it was neither a
story about how sensible actors should make decisions nor
a story about how the decisions of these actors might interact to produce a particular outcome. The tradition was, in
fact, exasperatingly blurry about who was making what
decisions, and almost completely silent on the question of
how decisions of individuals might affect one another.

Consider, for example, the famous problem of locating a
factory so as to minimize transportation costs from several
suppliers and to several markets. Who is doing the minimizing? Is this factory owned by a private firm? If so, how

does it price? Does it face competitors, and if so what assumptions does it make about their reactions? And in any case, why must there be only one production site—are there economies of scale so large that this is optimal, and what does that in turn say about market structure? One can only presume that the problem of transport cost minimization is embedded in some larger context—that there is an implicit story about pricing (which among other things will determine demand), competition, and market structure, one piece of which is the problem of minimizing transport costs given the decision to ship particular quantities to particular markets. This problem is interesting, but it stops so far short of what we usually want to do in economic models, being neither a full analysis of maximization nor even a partial equilibrium analysis, that it is deeply unsatisfying.

Central-place theory is in many ways a more satisfying piece of intellectual apparatus. It does tell a story about how individual agents interact—namely, that the trade-off between economies of scale and transportation costs leads producers to cluster together into a hierarchy of cities serving nested, hexagonal market areas. But on closer inspection it becomes unclear exactly what is supposed to be going on. Who is making the location decisions? Lösch seems to have proposed his hexagons as an optimum rather than a market outcome. Christaller was clearly talking about market outcomes, but without any clear description of market structure. Central-place theory thus provided a sort of schematic, a way to organize your thoughts and your data about urban systems, rather than an economic model in which the observed structure could be explained in terms of some deeper causes.

But why didn't some clever economist in the Anglo-Saxon tradition pick up central-place theory and produce a formal model? For some length of time, say up to the mid-1950s, simple ignorance can be the explanation: the German location tradition was simply not accessible to non-German-speaking theorists. After the proselytizing work of Isard and others, however, the essential ideas of central-place theory were there ready for theoretical elaboration. And indeed some very talented theorists did make attempts to formalize the framework. Yet these attempts did not succeed, at least as judged by the test of the intellectual marketplace.

Why? You know the answer: to make sense of central-place theory, one needs to deal with the problem of market structure. The idea is simple enough: each firm faces a trade-off between economies of scale, which push toward a limited number of production sites, and transport costs, which can be reduced by multiplying the number of sites. But this description immediately implies that we are in a world in which there are unexhausted economies of scale, and thus in a world of imperfect competition. You can't tell a complete story about central-place formation unless you are prepared to offer some description, however stylized, of that imperfectly competitive market structure. And that, until relatively recently, was something economists felt unable to do.

Let me make clear that all this is not meant as a condemnation of those who developed and elaborated central-place theory. On the contrary, they should be celebrated for the inspired and productive insights they achieved in spite of their inability to formalize their ideas effectively. But central-place theory will not truly come into its own until the formalization barrier is crossed.

Social Physics

The imagery of Germanic geometry is that of eighteenth-century mechanics: the problem of location was represented directly, as a matter of balancing several discrete forces of attraction. Weber's location problem can actually be solved by building a system of weights and pulleys. In the nineteenth century, however, it became increasingly common for physicists to represent their problems not directly, as the interacting influence of several different mechanical elements on each other, but indirectly, as the solution to some maximum or minimum problem. It turned out that many physical systems could be thought of as minimizing a quantity called "action," a formulation that greatly simplified analysis. It also turned out that dynamics could often be usefully represented as a movement of a point representing the system to locations of minimum potential on an imaginary surface. It was inevitable that the imagery of these physical concepts would eventually be reflected in thinking about economic geography. As it turned out, the school that developed along these lines emerged in the United States after World War II.

The idea of doing geography by analogy with physics was not a foolish one. Those of us who are deeply indoctrinated in the tradition of neoclassical economic analysis may be tempted to scoff—why not try to build up the story from economic foundations? But neoclassical theory was, as we've already seen, conspicuously unhelpful at this point in the development of spatial analysis, so one could hardly be blamed for trying something different.

Also, American geographers who began to look at the data on cities quickly noticed that there were striking empirical regularities in that data, of the kind that physical scientists are accustomed to seeing but that are rarely seen in economics. I can't resist showing you one example: Zipf's law, otherwise known as the rank-size rule. The "law" is an assertion about the distribution of city sizes, taking the form

$$N_j = \frac{k}{R_j^{b'}}$$

where N is the population of city j, R its rank (so that for the United States, New York is 1, Los Angeles 2, Chicago 3, and so on), and b is an exponent close to 1. In hard science one is always finding relations like this, which then serve as a challenge for theorists. In social science they are rare. But just look at it (see figure 2.1).

By the way, if you think that I am going to wrap up this lecture by showing how modern theory can explain Zipf's

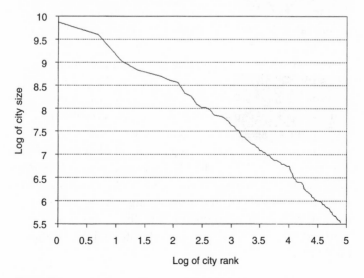

Figure 2.1

law, you're going to be disappointed. I think I may have
the ghostly beginnings of an explanation, but at this point
we have to say that the rank-size rule is a major embarrassment for economic theory: one of the strongest statistical
relationships we know, lacking any clear basis in theory.

Another physics-like relationship is the "gravity law" re-
lating interactions between cities—travel, shipments, etc.—
to the populations and the distance between them. This
"law" takes the form

$$T_{ij} = k \frac{N_i N_j}{D_{ij}^b},$$

where T is the volume of transactions between the cities, D
is the distance between them, and b is again an exponent—
possibly close to one, although there is more dispute in this
case. The gravity law doesn't work quite as astonishingly
as the rank-size rule, but it's still a pretty good fit; and like
the rank-size rule it has proved extremely useful as a way
to look at data, both in spatial economics and in international trade.

But how can the observation that spatial economics ex-
hibits physics-like relationships, and the desire of geographers to be more like real scientists, give rise to anything
that looks like a causal as opposed to descriptive theory?
Well, in the 1950s American geographers came up with the
idea that firms tend, other things equal, to choose locations
of maximum "market potential," where the market potential of a site was defined as some index of its access to markets, involving both the purchasing power of all the
markets to which it might sell and the distance to those
markets. A typical index of market potential for location i
might be

$$P_i = \Sigma_j \, k \frac{Y_j}{D_{ij}^b},$$

where Y is the income or purchasing power of a particular market. The relationship to the gravity model is obvious. But aside from that sort-of-formal justification, it is not hard to believe that some index along these lines ought to be at least helpful in understanding where firms locate-after all, surely it is in fact the case that firms try to locate where access to markets, defined somehow or other, is good.

Now it turns out that market potential does indeed "work," in the sense that indices of market potential do seem to have quite a lot of power to explain the location of industry across the United States (or Western Europe) and the location of particular activities within urban areas. (In the 1950s Harris [1954] and others drew striking maps of market potential surfaces for the United States, which showed a clear correlation between high market potential and the concentration of industry in the manufacturing belt. More recently, market potential studies for the European Commission have led to similar maps that show a clear relationship between "centrality" and per capita income.) And unlike the rigid structure of Weberian location theory, the market potential approach lends itself readily to application.

So here is a puzzle: the "social physics" approach to spatial economics offers plausible stories, some striking empirical regularities, and a useful basis for empirical work. It can even be used as the basis for some ad hoc equilibrium models, as I'll describe later. So why isn't this approach part of the economist's standard toolbox?

You know the answer. But let me point out the specific problem: it is completely unclear what is being maximized when a firm chooses a point of maximum market potential. Indeed, if you think about it at all you realize that the whole idea of computing market potential in the way that I have described must implicitly involve some strong beliefs about market structure. Firms cannot exhibit constant returns to scale—otherwise one would simply establish a facility to serve every market, and there would be no reason to compute a single market potential surface for the whole of the United States or the European Union. Nor can they be producing goods that are perfect substitutes; there would be sharply defined market areas after the manner of Lösch, not smooth potential surfaces with no edges. Thus the market potential approach seems to have an implicit monopolistic competition story lurking underneath—but that story is entirely implicit, and had to be so, since monopolistic competition was not something people knew how to model during the heyday of the market potential approach.

Cumulative Causation

One immediately obvious implication of the market potential analysis is the possibility of circularity. Firms want to locate where market potential is high, that is, near large markets. But markets will tend to be large where lots of firms locate. So one is led naturally to a consideration of the possibility of self-reinforcing regional growth or decline.

I am not entirely clear on how well geographers understood this point. The pioneering paper by Harris (1954) certainly pointed out that regions with high market potential, such as the U.S. manufacturing belt, would find their advantage reinforced as more firms were induced to move there. Whether the possibility of multiple equilibria was really appreciated at first is less clear.

A case in point was the pioneering modeling effort by Lowry (1964). Lowry produced something that was remarkably ahead of its time: a calibrated numerical model of land use within a city (Pittsburgh) in which many location decisions were endogenous, and in which implicit increasing returns implied multiple equilibria. Lowry's model was not based on maximizing behavior—it could not have been, given the state of the modeling art at that time. Instead, he imposed a set of plausible, ad hoc rules. Location decisions by firms, in particular, were based largely on market potential.

This was, to repeat, a remarkable and pioneering effort. And yet there are signs that Lowry himself did not fully understand what he was up to. In particular, there is a giveaway remark in which he says that it is crucial to solve the equations in the right order—if they are solved in the wrong order, they give different answers! In other words, he regarded the multiple equilibria in his model as a nuisance, not as an insight into the process of spatial development.

But if the geographers who worked with market potential may not have been entirely clear-minded about the possibility of circularity, there were other geographers who were very aware of that possibility, for a very good reason: they were sitting at the feet of the creators of high development theory.

Consider the story of multiple equilibria I have just told, in which firms locate where markets are large, but markets are large where firms locate. Isn't this essentially the same as the Big Push story of development, in which firms adopt modern techniques if the market is sufficiently large, but the market is sufficiently large if enough firms adopt modern techniques? Of course it is; and so it was natural to carry over concepts from high development theory into economic geography.

Indeed, I would argue that the ideas of high development theory are more plausible in a locational context than they are in their original habitat. The Big Push model in its original version relied crucially on the availability of an elastic supply of labor from a low-wage rural sector; yet the wage differentials of the surplus labor story were never really explained, merely asserted. It was possible to surmount this difficulty by invoking very strong linkages involving intermediate goods, but even sympathetic observers may wonder whether, given the inelasticity of factor supply that is all too likely in many developing countries, the multiple equilibria of Big Push-type stories are really plausible.

In economic geography, however, the supply of factors *to any one region or location* will typically be very elastic, because they can come from someplace else. And so while a Big Push for the economy as a whole may be implausible, a Big Snowball for a particular region may make perfectly good sense.

Some of the authors of the classic high development tracts seem to have realized this. Certainly Myrdal illustrated his concept of "circular and cumulative causation" with regional examples first, and Hirschman also liked to talk about unequal regional development within a country. The explicit application of high development concepts to regional growth, however, is something one usually associates with Alan Pred (1966).

Pred's story is essentially a variant on the Big Push. Suppose that a regional economy grows to the critical point at which it becomes profitable to replace imports of some good subject to scale economies with local production. This import substitution will expand regional employment, drawing in workers from other regions; and in so doing will further expand the local market. This market expansion may, in turn, provide the market size necessary to induce a second round of import substitution, and so on— a cascade of growth reflecting the circular relationship between market size and the range of industries that a region possesses.

The story can, of course, be elaborated. In particular, if you add forward as well as backward linkages, the growth need not be solely due to import substitution, but may involve some export growth as well. But surely the basic idea is very clear.

What is not clear, however, is—well, you know. Pred's discussion is conspicuously silent on the question of market structure. And as a result what he and his followers call a "model" is hardly something a modern economist would recognize as such: it is merely a set of boxes and arrows, suggesting relationships without being at all clear about how they work.

Local External Economies

Let me now turn to a tradition that is much closer to mainstream economics, indeed one that is essentially a part of the mainstream if not a very major one: the analysis of local external economies.

The idea that clustering of producers in a particular location yields advantages, and that these advantages in turn explain such clustering, is an old one. I don't know who first pointed it out, but the economist who made the most of it was none other than Alfred Marshall. Indeed, to those who imagine that increasing returns are something only recently discovered, it is startling to see how much attention is given in Marshall's *Principles* to local externalities. They are emphasized both for their intrinsic importance and for the way they exemplify his concept of external economies in general.

What Marshall meant by an external economy was not exactly what later authors meant. In the 1940s and 1950s economists came to make a clear distinction between technological external economies—pure spillovers—and pecuniary externalities mediated through the market. In a world of constant returns at the level of the firm and perfect competition, pecuniary externalities don't have any particular importance, so only technological spillovers matter. Marshall, however, did not make this distinction. He lumped together the ability of a large local market to support efficient-scale suppliers of intermediate inputs, the advantages of a thick labor market, and the information exchange that takes place when firms in the same industry cluster together—two pecuniary externalities, one technological. In the light of current theory, of course, he was right to do so. We now understand that the sharp distinction between technological and pecuniary external economies holds only in a constant-returns world; in general market-size external economies are just as real as technical spillovers.

Even if Marshall did not restrict his discussion to "pure" external economies, however, it was certainly possible to do Marshallian analysis with such pure external economies—and in so doing, to make use of the apparatus of individual maximization and competitive equilibrium that economists were coming to understand ever better. Thus local external economies never disappeared as a concept from economics. Indeed, if you were to ask a mainstream economist at any time between, say, 1930 and the last few years why cities exist, or why some industries are so concentrated in space, he or she would surely answer in terms of just such local externalities.

One can go further, and mainstream economists did. Suppose that we think of positive local external economies, which tend to promote concentration of production, as being opposed by other effects—congestion or land costs—that tend to promote dispersal. Then we are on our way toward a story about both the optimal size of cities and, if we are prepared to make some assumptions about the process of city formation, a theory of the actual size and number of cities. An elegant model along these lines was laid out by Vernon Henderson in 1974, and Henderson's urban system model has become the basis for a large literature, including a considerable amount of useful empirical work.

And yet while the idea of external economies has always been respectable—indeed recognized as essential by any sensible economist who thought about it—it has been surprisingly neglected in our economic tradition. If you consider the intrinsic importance of urban external economies as a real-world issue, and then look at the actual attention they get from economists, it is obvious that there is a major mismatch. Why?

My own guess is that while it has been possible to make the sources of agglomeration safe for neoclassical economics by assuming that they are pure technological externalities, this strategic evasion has been costly in terms of both credibility and researchability. To say that urbanization is the result of localized external economies carries more than a hint of Molière's doctor, who explained that opium induces sleep thanks to its dormitive properties. Or as a sarcastic physicist remarked to an economist at one inter-disciplinary meeting, "So what you're saying is that firms agglomerate because of agglomeration effects." Moreover, the pure-externality assumption puts these effects into a kind of black box, where nothing more can be said. Oh, you can try to measure them empirically, and there has been some important work along those lines. But you have no deeper structure to examine, no way to relate agglomer-ation to more micro-level features of the economy.

Land Rent and Land Use

We finally come to the last of my five traditions: the analy-sis of land rent and land use, deriving directly from von Thünen and his pioneering *Isolated State*.

Von Thünen's idea is, by now, thoroughly familiar to almost all economists—although even this analysis is ne-glected in the principles textbooks. He envisaged an agri-cultural plain supplying a variety of products to an isolated central city; and he realized that one could think of the si-multaneous determination of a land rent gradient declin-ing from the center to an outer limit of cultivation, and of a series of rings in which different crops would be cultivated and/or different farming methods adopted. Thus the high-rent land near the center would be reserved for crops with high costs of transportation and/or crops yielding high value per acre; the outermost ring would consist of either land-intensive or cheaply transported crops.

If one judges the importance of an idea by the amount of work it has inspired, then von Thünen's contribution far outweighs any other tradition in spatial economics. Mark Blaug devotes almost half of his review of spatial economics to von Thünen and his successors—and even this does not take account of the influence of von Thünen-based models in the analysis of the *internal structure* of urban areas, which I turn to below. Von Thünen has attracted favorable attention from many modern economists, from Herbert Giersch to Paul Samuelson.

All of this is in many ways amply justified. The von Thünen model (even if it was Launhardt who really first got it right) is a beautiful thing. It illustrates in a surprising context many of the key concepts of neoclassical economics: the idea of equilibrium; the idea that "value" does not inhere in some hidden essence, but is instead an *emergent* consequence of a market process (would that Marx had read von Thünen); the simultaneous determination of goods and factor prices; the ability of markets to achieve efficient outcomes; and the role of prices, even for nonproduced, "undeserving" factors like land, in providing the incentives that promote efficiency.

The one thing that the von Thünen model does not tell you much about, unfortunately, is the central issue of spatial economics. Or let me be more precise: if you regard it as essential that you be able to understand why and how the economy avoids "backyard capitalism," the von Thünen model provides absolutely no help. It simply assumes the thing you want to understand: the existence of a central urban market. Indeed, the whole thrust of the model is to understand the forces that spread economic activity *away* from that center, the "centrifugal" forces if you will. About the "centripetal" forces that *create* centers, that pull economic activity together, it can and does say nothing.

Why should a model with such a powerful limitation bulk so large in location theory? Why, in particular, should

a model that at best treats half the question have received
so much more attention than other approaches that made a
pretty good stab at answering the other half? The answer,
of course, is that while the approaches I have described up
to this point may have been insightful, they offered no opportunity for economists to make use of the tools they had.
By contrast, the von Thünen model might almost have
been designed as a showpiece for the power of the competitive, constant-returns paradigm.

Two parallels should immediately be obvious. First, von
Thünen was to economic geography what the Lewis sur-
plus-labor model was to development. That is, it was the
one piece of a heterodox framework that could easily be
handled with orthodox methods, and so it attracted research effort out of all proportion to its considerable mer-
its. (This parallel presumes that the other approaches I
have described add up to a common framework, which
may be not at all obvious at this point; but I'll argue in a little while that they do.)

Second, the focus on the von Thünen approach is remi-
niscent of the attitudes of geologists in the era before the
discovery of seafloor spreading. They understood erosion,
which tears mountains down, while lacking a model for
understanding how they get built up—and thus the core of
geological theory was the loving analysis of erosion by water, wind, and ice. Economists understood why economic
activity spreads out, not why it becomes concentrated—
and thus the central model of spatial economics became
one that deals only with the way that competition for land
drives economic activities away from a central market.

There is, however, only so much that you can say about
concentric rings of land use. As much as the von Thünen
model may have met with the approval of mainstream

economists, it was not enough to sustain a vital field. And so spatial economics languished along the periphery of economics proper.

What economic geography needed—and still needs—in order to be revitalized is a synthesis that brings back the other half of the story. It needs something that will legitimize and make sense of the insights of the outcast approaches.

I believe that we now have the intellectual tools to create that synthesis. But I am not the first one to think so. So let me digress for a bit to talk about two valiant but failed efforts to bring space into the economic mainstream.

Spatial Economics: Two Failed Efforts

I guess it's obvious, both from what I've said so far in these lectures and from other things I've written, that I believe that economic geography's time has come, that we are ready to put spatial concerns into the mainstream of economics. But history scoffs at my optimism. At least twice in the period since World War II it seemed that spatial economics was about to break into the big time. Yet in both cases the wave broke well short of the beach.

The first big effort to get space into economics came in the 1950s, under the leadership of the redoubtable Walter Isard. Isard was and is a man of huge energy and vast learning; he performed an invaluable service in making the previously inaccessible German tradition available to monolingual economists like myself; and he created an interdisciplinary enterprise, regional science, which has been of considerable practical importance in the real world. But the aim he set himself in his magnum opus, *Location and Space-Economy*, to bring spatial concerns into the heart of economic theory, was never attained.

Why? One hesitates to criticize an economist of Isard's eminence—just as one hesitates to second-guess an Albert Hirschman. Yet it seems to me at least that Isard, for all his learning and acumen, failed to understand just what it was that had kept space out of the economic literature.

Location and Space-Economy was in large part a work of synthesis, assembling von Thünen and Weber, Christaller and Lösch into a manageable package. Isard's principal original contribution was to reformulate the problem of location as a standard problem of substitution: firms, he argued, could be viewed as trading off transportation costs against production costs just as they make any other cost-minimizing or profit-maximizing decision-a perfectly correct observation. But Isard's conclusion from this observation was that one could therefore simply view location as another choice variable in a general equilibrium competitive model, of the kind that was coming to dominate economic analysis. And this was simply wrong: to make any sense of the various approaches to location that he surveyed, one must take account of increasing returns and hence of imperfect competition. Isard never actually presented an example of a general locational equilibrium; this was no accident, because neither he nor anyone else at that time knew how to do so.

In effect, Isard was saying to economists, "Look! You can deal with space using the tools you already have!" But they couldn't—and so his project was doomed to failure.

Luckily for Isard and for the world, that was not the end of the story. The half-worked-out spatial models he provided made almost no dent in economic theory, but they were undeniably useful for a variety of practical purposes: a regional planner trying to decide where to build roads or ports may be willing to settle for a set of schematic or sug-

gestive intellectual devices that fall well short of an intellectually satisfying or coherent structure, as long as it helps
her frame her problem a bit better. Instead of a deep body
of theoretical work, what Isard ended up creating was an
eclectic applied field: regional science. Regional science is
not a unified subject. It is best described as a collection of
tools, some crude, some fairly sophisticated, which can
help someone who needs an answer to practical problems
involving spatial issues that will not wait until we have a
good theory.

I would argue that economists should give this kind of
loose-jointed, do-the-best-you-can theorizing more attention and respect than we do. But at the same time, the kind
of eclecticism that marks regional science is no substitute
for a truly integrated theory; and Isard's great effort failed
to achieve that integration.[2]

The second big effort to bring space into economics was
more modest in its goals, and correspondingly far more
successful in its initial entry into the field; yet in the end it,
too, failed. I refer to the "new urban economics" that flourished in the late 1960s and early 1970s. This was a literature
that concerned itself with the internal spatial structure of
cities. The canonical model was of a monocentric city, in
which at least some fraction of the population was obliged
to commute to an exogenously given central business district. The problem was then to determine simultaneously
the pattern of land use and land rents around that central
business district, a problem that generally reduced itself to
the determination of an equilibrium bid-rent curve as a
function of distance from the center.

Does this sound familiar? Of course it does: it is pure
von Thünen, with commuters instead of farmers. And the
new models shared many of the virtues of the original von

Thünen model: they offered a deeply satisfying picture of how market forces trade off access for land, of how space becomes structured into zones characterized by different activities, of the simultaneity, the general equilibrium, that characterizes economics when there is competition for scarce resources.

Unfortunately, the new models also shared the basic vice of von Thünen: the (literally) central fact, the existence of a central business district around which the city was organized, was left uncomfortably unexplained. One could, of course, appeal to loosely specified agglomeration economies to complete the model, but that was not a very satisfying closure. Worse yet, it became increasingly inadequate because the real world decided to play a nasty trick on the modelers, by abolishing the monocentric city as a reasonable approximation.

Anyone who has driven around an American metropolitan area knows what I am talking about. The quintessential city of America in 1950 was Chicago, a city built on railroads and exemplifying the centralization that rail transport fosters. Chicago in 1950 was clearly centered on the Loop, the famous, densely packed office district that was the original home of the skyscraper. Even now it is, urban geographers tell me, the most monocentric city remaining in the United States. But Chicago is no longer the number-two city. Its place has been taken by Los Angeles, the city Gertrude Stein described as having "no there there." LA is not, whatever Ms. Stein may have thought, an undifferentiated mass: neighborhoods are sharply distinct in terms of character and land use. But there is no single center: a dozen or more office districts compete with each other.

Those of us from the "real" cities of the East and Midwest used to scoff at Los Angeles. Nowadays, however, the fact is that most of us for all practical purposes live and work in LA-like environments. Most of my friends in the Boston area work for the high-technology companies along Route 128; they commute *outward* from their inner-suburb homes to the "edge cities" that have grown up around Boston, as they have around every old U.S. metropolis.

The point is, of course, that the von Thünen ring scheme sheds at best a very dim light on the spatial structure of polycentric cities. What we need to understand, first and foremost, is where the competing centers are located—precisely the question that von Thünen-type models avoid answering. And the reason they do not answer it is, in turn, because it is a question that is inevitably intimately bound up with increasing returns.[3]

Into the Mainstream

Up to this point I have been telling tales of frustration; of sensible ideas that could not be effectively formalized, or of formalizable ideas that seem to have missed the point. Now I want to explain why I believe that this will all have a happy ending.

The essential reason for optimism is that economists now have at their disposal some new tools. It used to be that as soon as you tried to deal with any question involving economies of scale at the level of the individual firm, you were either restricted to studying pure monopoly or to a handful of awkward duopoly models. Above all, there was no way that you could speak about general equilibrium. This situation has not completely changed: there are still no *general* models of economies characterized by increasing returns and imperfect competition, or for that matter even any models that are plausible in detail. If you are the kind of person who balks at silly assumptions made for analytical convenience, you will not be encouraged by the picture I am about to paint. But we do now have a set of modeling tricks that allow us at least to present illustrative examples of economies subject to increasing returns.

You've already seen an example of these tricks in the first lecture, where I showed how Murphy et al. used a simple model of symmetric, limit-pricing monopolists to cut through the confusions of the Big Push story. Not everyone is happy with this kind of analytical sleight of hand: I have heard that at least one Nobel laureate reacted to their paper with an angry dismissal, saying "it can't be that simple." To my taste, however, Murphy et al. provided exactly what we needed: a simple, clear illustration that all at once makes what Rosenstein-Rodan was saying completely comprehensible.

For the problems of spatial economics, that particular trick won't do, for reasons not worth describing—let's just say that I have tried quite hard to do it, and I am pretty sure there isn't any way. But there are other tricks. The one that I have found most useful is the formalization of monopolistic competition suggested in 1977 by Dixit and Stiglitz—a completely unrealistic model, but one that I (and many other theorists in international trade, growth, and other fields) have found fabulously useful for constructing clarifying examples.

Over the last few years I have been gradually constructing a model of a spatial economy that relies on the Dixit-Stiglitz approach to monopolistic competition to "sterilize" the problem of imperfect competition. I do not claim that this approach is the only way to do spatial economics, or even that it is a wholly satisfactory model. What I do claim is that the model demonstrates the feasibility of telling the kind of stories that are needed to do meaningful economic geography in a way that mainstream economists can live with.

The formal model is given in the appendix. All that we need to talk about now are a few general aspects of the approach. I imagine an economy with a number of separate locations. (It is possible to deal with a continuum of locations as well; indeed, there are some very interesting ways of looking at agglomeration in a continuous spatial economy, but I won't go into them here.) There are two sectors: agriculture, which is geographically immobile, and manufacturing, which is mobile over time. The geographic reallocation of manufacturing is, however, not instantaneous; it turns out to be important to introduce at least a rudimentary story about dynamics.

Manufacturing consists of many firms producing differentiated products; increasing returns ensure that not all potential goods are produced, and thus that each plant produces a unique good (thereby justifying the Weber assumption that each good is produced at a single location). The monopolistic competition assumption neatly, if implausibly, disposes of problems like strategic behavior. All that firms need to do is choose an optimal location, taking into account the spatial distribution of demand and the transportation costs they must pay.

The way I've described it, the model doesn't sound like much. Actually, it is remarkably hard to come up with a formal structure that simultaneously includes increasing returns and the resulting imperfect competition, transportation costs, and factor mobility—and that you can still work with. But anyway, I have such a structure. What does it tell me?

The most important thing I learned is that all of my first four traditions in spatial analysis—Germanic geometry (specifically central-place theory), social physics (specifically the market potential approach), cumulative causation, and localized external economies—make perfectly good sense in terms of a rigorous economic model. They don't come out exactly the way their originators presented them, but the basic insights stand up quite well.

Moreover, it turns out that all four traditions are really different aspects of the same story—different ways of looking at the same thing. This may not be too surprising an insight about traditions 2, 3, and 4. Consider first a snapshot of my model economy at a point in time, which is to say with some given distribution of manufacturing across space. We will, of course, find that some locations are more desirable for manufacturing than others. And we will not be surprised to find that the desirability of sites can be measured by a market potential index that is rather more complicated than the ones used by the social physicists but still recognizably related.

Next consider how the economy evolves. Manufacturing will move toward more desirable sites and away from less desirable ones, but in so doing it will change the market potential map, typically reinforcing the advantage of already-favored locations. Thus market potential becomes part of a story of circular and cumulative causation.

Finally, the clustering of production that results from this dynamic process can be seen as the consequence of a kind of pecuniary external economy, not really inconsistent with Marshall's description.

What may seem more obscure is how central-place theory could fit into the same scheme. Indeed, it does not fit quite as easily, partly because central-place theory is often expressed as if central places served only the demands of an evenly spread farm population. If you think about it, of course, central places must also serve the markets they provide for themselves and for each other, which already starts to sound a bit more like what I have already described. But can anything like the regular spacing of centers imagined by Christaller and Lösch emerge from the cumulative processes of Pred?

The initially surprising answer is yes. I have carried out a number of simulation experiments with a highly stylized economy in which locations are lined up symmetrically around a circle. For each simulation I began with a random allocation of manufacturing across locations, then let the economy evolve. For some parameter values, of course, all manufacturing ends up in a single location. When the parameters are such that several manufacturing centers typically emerge, however, they are normally roughly evenly spaced around the circle. That is, this linear economy spontaneously organizes itself into a pattern of central places with roughly equal-sized market areas.

I have a pretty good idea of why this is true, but haven't got it fully worked out yet. Let's just say that "successful" locations, those that end up with a lot of manufacturing, tend to cast an "agglomeration shadow" over nearby locations, but that rival centers can thrive if they are far enough apart; the result is thus a number of centers at a more or less characteristic distance. Some work in progress suggests to me that the spacing will be more regular, the smoother the initial distribution of manufacturing, with an almost perfectly smooth initial distribution producing a perfect central-place pattern in which the distance between centers is determined by the parameters of the model.

All this is for a one-dimensional economy, but I am, as Michael Milken would say, highly confident that the same model extended to two dimensions would produce a lattice of central places with hexagonal market areas: Lösch vindicated. I am less confident but hopeful that in a model with two or more manufacturing sectors characterized by different scale economies or transport costs the approach will yield Christaller-type hierarchies. I even have a fantasy that in a many-sector model there will emerge some deep justification for the rank-size rule, though that may be too much to hope for.

The Moral of the Story

As you can no doubt tell, I am excited by all of this. But while it was important for me to explain at least briefly the kind of formalization that, to me at least, makes sense of all these spatial economic traditions, the point for these lectures is not to emphasize the specific models that make up my current research. The point is, instead, to realize that in economic geography as in development economics, the unwillingness of mainstream economists to think about what they could not formalize led them to ignore ideas that turn out, in retrospect, to have been very good ones. Central-place theory is a powerful organizing principle for looking at and thinking about urban systems—and in only slightly modified form it turns out to make sense in terms of a rigorous economic model. Market potential is an extremely useful empirical concept for measuring market access—and it too, in slightly modified form, turns out to make sense in terms of a rigorous model. Circular and cumulative causation is a compelling image that helps you to think about the evolution of regional economies—and it is eminently sensible in terms of modern economic models. Yet all of these ideas were essentially exiled from economic theory, if they were ever allowed in in the first place. The only piece of spatial economics to gain real mainstream acceptance, von Thünen's land-use model, is a thing of beauty; but surely its appeal was more a matter of tractability than of power to explain the world.

So what's the moral? We've seen how the insistence on models that meet the standards of rigor in mainstream economics can lead to neglect of clearly valuable ideas. Does this mean that the whole emphasis on models is wrong? Should we make a major effort to open up economics, to relax our standards about what constitutes an acceptable argument?

No—the moral of my tale is nowhere near that easy. Economists can often be remarkably obtuse, failing to see things that are right in front of them. But sometimes a bit of obtuseness is not entirely a bad thing.

3 Models and Metaphors

In the previous two lectures I offered personal views of the history of thought in two fields that were strangely unsuccessful in influencing mainstream thought in economics. Development economics, or more specifically the set of ideas that I call "high development theory," had a huge initial influence. But it then faded away, virtually disappearing from economic discourse. Economic geography never really got its foot inside the door—to this day the silence of standard economics on such subjects as the location, size, or even existence of cities is startling.

In each case, I have argued, the basic problem was one neither of ignorance nor of bias. Economists did not abandon the insights of development economics because they had forgotten about the subject; they did not ignore the ideas of the geographers because to acknowledge space would somehow conflict with free-market prejudices. No, these fields were left untilled because the terrain was seen as unsuitable for the tools at hand. Economists realized that they could not model Big Push development or almost anything interesting about economic geography with the kind of rigor that was increasingly expected of them, and so they simply left the subjects alone.

This surely sounds like an indictment of the economics profession. Here were interesting, basically sensible ideas, ideas that made sense to anyone who did *not* have professional training in economics. And yet because they could not be modeled with the rigor required by the increasingly narrow standards of the journals, they were ignored. Doesn't this say that we have made a fetish of formalism? Doesn't it even seem to imply that the whole profession may have taken a wrong turning?

No: while many economists are indeed too narrow-minded, the insistence on models is right, even when it sometimes leads us unfairly to overlook good ideas. To understand why, we need to stop for a little while and ask why we need formal economic models in the first place.

The Benefits—and Costs—of Models

I have just acknowledged that the tendency of economists to emphasize what they know how to model formally can create blind spots; yet I have also claimed that the insistence on modeling is basically right. What I want to do now is call a time out and discuss more broadly the role of models in intellectual inquiry.

It is said that those who can, do, while those who cannot, discuss methodology. So the very fact that I raise the issue of methodology in these lectures tells you something about the state of economics. Yet in some ways the problems of economics and of social science in general are part of a broader methodological problem that afflicts many fields: how to deal with complex systems.

It is in a way unfortunate that for many of us the image of a successful field of scientific endeavor is basic physics.

The objective of the most basic physics is a complete description of what happens. In principle and apparently in practice, quantum mechanics gives a complete account of what goes on inside, say, a hydrogen atom. But most things we want to analyze, even in physical science, cannot be dealt with at that level of completeness. The only exact model of the global weather system is that system itself. Any smaller-scale model of that system is therefore to some degree a falsification: it leaves out many aspects of reality.

How, then, does the meteorological researcher decide what to put into his model? And how does he decide whether his model is a good one? The answer to the first question is that the choice of model represents a mixture of judgment and compromise. The model must be something you know how to make—that is, you are constrained by your modeling techniques. And the model must be something you can construct given your resources—time, money, and patience are not unlimited. There may be a wide variety of models possible given those constraints; which one or ones you choose actually to build depends on educated guessing.

And how do you know that the model is good? It will never be *right* in the way that quantum electrodynamics is right. At a certain point you may be good enough at predicting that your results can be put to repeated practical use, like the giant weather-forecasting models that run on today's supercomputers; in that case predictive success can be measured in terms of dollars and cents, and the improvement of models becomes a quantifiable matter. In the early stages of a complex science, however, the criterion for a good model is more subjective: it is a good model if it succeeds in explaining or rationalizing some of what you see in the world in a way that you might not have expected.

Notice that I have not specified exactly what I mean by a model. You may think that I must mean a mathematical model, perhaps a computer simulation. And indeed that's mostly what we have to work with in economics. But a model can equally well be a physical one, and I'd like to describe briefly an example from the pre-computer era of meteorological research: Fultz's dishpan.[1]

Dave Fultz was a researcher at the University of Chicago in the early postwar years, who sought an answer to what might seem a very hard question: what factors are essential to generating the intricacy and variability of world weather? Is it a process that depends on the full complexity of the world—the interaction of ocean currents and the atmosphere, the location of mountain ranges, the alternation of the seasons, and so on—or does the basic pattern of weather, for all its complexity, have simple roots?

He was able to show the essential simplicity of the weather's causes with a "model" that consisted of a dishpan filled with water, placed on a slowly rotating turntable, with an electric heating element bent around the outside of the pan. Aluminum flakes and dye were suspended in the water, so that a camera perched overhead and rotating with the pan could take pictures of the pattern of flow.

The setup was designed to reproduce two features of the global weather system: the temperature differential between the poles and the equator, and the Coriolis force that results from the earth's spin. Everything else—all the rich detail of the actual planet—was suppressed. And yet the dishpan exhibited steady flows near the rim that clearly corresponded to the tropical trade winds, great eddies that were just about the size (relative to the pan) and the shape of the cyclonic storms of the temperate regions, even a twisting ribbon of fast-flowing water that unmistakably corresponded to the only recently discovered jet stream. Fultz's dishpan, without a doubt, showed the essential elements of actual weather.

What did one learn from the dishpan? It was not telling an entirely true story: the earth is not flat, air is not water, the real world has oceans and mountain ranges and for that matter two hemispheres. The unrealism of the model world was dictated by what atmospheric theorists were able to or could be bothered to build—in effect, by the limitations of their modeling technique. Nonetheless, the model did convey a powerful insight into why the weather system behaves the way it does.

The important point is that any kind of model of a complex system—a physical model, a computer simulation, or a pencil-and-paper mathematical representation— amounts to pretty much the same kind of procedure. You make a set of clearly untrue simplifications to get the system down to something you can handle; those simplifications are dictated partly by guesses about what is important, partly by the modeling techniques available. And the end result, if the model is a good one, is an improved insight into why the vastly more complex real system behaves the way it does.

But there are also costs. The strategic omissions involved in building a model almost always involve throwing away some real information. Oceans and mountain ranges *do* affect the earth's weather, even if they are hard to put in a dishpan. And yet once you have a model, it is essentially impossible to avoid seeing the world in terms of that model—which means focusing on the forces and effects your model can represent and ignoring or giving short shrift to those it cannot. The result is that the very act of modeling has the effect of destroying knowledge as well as creating it. A successful model enhances our vision, but it also creates blind spots, at least at first.

The cycle of knowledge lost before it can be regained seems to be an inevitable part of formal model-building. Here's another story from meteorology. Folk wisdom has always said that you can predict future weather from the aspect of the sky, and had claimed that certain kinds of clouds presaged storms. As meteorology developed in the nineteenth and early twentieth centuries, however—as it made such fundamental discoveries, completely unknown to folk wisdom, as the fact that the winds in a storm blow in a circular path—it basically stopped paying attention to how the sky looked. Serious students of the weather studied wind direction and barometric pressure, not the pretty patterns made by condensing water vapor. It was not until 1919 that a group of Norwegian scientists realized that the folk wisdom had been right all along—that one could identify the onset and development of a cyclonic storm quite accurately by looking at the shapes and altitude of the cloud cover.

The point is not that a century of research into the weather had only reaffirmed what everyone knew from the beginning. The meteorology of 1919 had learned many things of which folklore was unaware, and dispelled many myths. Nor is the point that meteorologists somehow sinned by not looking at clouds for so long. What happened was simply inevitable: during the process of model-building, there is a narrowing of vision imposed by the limitations of one's framework and tools, a narrowing that can only be ended definitively by making those tools good enough to transcend those limitations.

All of this is, I suppose, fairly uncontroversial when we are talking about understanding natural systems like the weather. But what happens when we turn to social systems, like the economy? Then many people suddenly adopt a very different attitude.

Modeling in Economics

When it comes to physical science, few people have problems with the idea that to study complex systems it is necessary to build simplified models. When we turn to social science, however, the whole issue of modeling begins to raise people's hackles. Suddenly the idea of representing the relevant system through a set of simplifications that are dictated at least in part by the available techniques becomes highly objectionable. Everyone accepts that it was reasonable for meteorologists to represent the earth, at least for a first pass, with a flat dish, because that was what was practical. But what do you think about the decision of most economists between 1820 and 1970 to represent the economy as a set of perfectly competitive markets, because a model of perfect competition was what they knew how to build? It's essentially the same thing, but it raises howls of indignation.

Why is our attitude so different when we come to social science? There are some discreditable reasons: like Victorians offended by the suggestion that they were descended from apes, some humanists imagine that their dignity is threatened when human society is represented as the moral equivalent of a dish on a turntable. Also, the most vociferous critics of economic models are often politically motivated. They have very strong ideas about what they want to believe; their convictions are essentially driven by values rather than analysis, but when an analysis threatens those beliefs they prefer to attack its assumptions rather than examine the basis for their own beliefs.

Still, there are more creditable reasons for disliking economic modeling, or at least the kind of models that make up mainstream economics. To many intelligent people the whole tone of economics seems strange and off-putting. On one side, there seems to be a near-total lack of social or psychological texture—economists are notoriously uninterested in how people actually think or feel. On the other side, there is what appears to most people to be a bristling mathematical complexity, with its accompanying strange jargon. Even someone who can accept that a dishpan tells us something about global weather may be totally unconvinced that a set of equations tells us anything useful about the global economy. There is a significant group of intellectuals who regard the whole mainstream tradition in economics as a kind of aberration, which will eventually be discarded; who regard all of us as, in the words of John Kenneth Galbraith, a "failed profession."

As you might guess, of course, I do not share that view. In fact, I would claim that the very things in the tradition of economics that most repel the layman are its greatest virtues. Economics is marked by a startling crudeness in the way it thinks about individuals and their motivations, yet it builds a huge structure on the basis of these simplistic foundations. Is this naive? No: it is in fact tremendously sophisticated.

At base, mainstream economic theory rests on two observations: obvious opportunities for gain are rarely left unexploited, and things add up. (Or as I sometimes put it,

$20 bills don't lie in plain view for very long, and every sale is also a purchase.) When one sets out to make a formal mathematical model, these rough principles usually become the more exact ideas of maximization (of something) and equilibrium (in some sense). It is, however, a good idea always to keep the looser statement in mind, for two opposing reasons—to remind yourself not to take any particular mathematical formalization too seriously, but also to remind yourself that the basic principles of mainstream economics are not at all silly or unreasonable.

What we do when we construct an economic model is to try to use those two principles to cut through the complexities of a situation. And the remarkable thing is how often that effort succeeds. Thinking carefully about how self-interested individuals would act in a particular situation, and how these actions would interact, can often produce powerful and surprising insights.

One cannot give a better example than the von Thünen model. To someone innocent of that model, the question of how land should be allocated among a variety of crops with different transportation costs and yields might seem a very complicated problem, whose solution requires a great deal of knowledge about the particulars. The question of how that land would actually be allocated in the marketplace might seem an entirely different problem, one which would require some historical and institutional knowledge of the particular society under discussion. And as for the question of how much the owners of land receive—well, that's surely a matter of power and class struggle, isn't it? Yet the basic principles of economics tell us that there is an unexpected order in the outcome, which is quite independent of the details. Obvious opportunities will not go unexploited: a farmer will bid away land from another

farmer if the extra rent is less than the saving in transportation cost, move to lower rent land if the reverse is true.
Things add up: the farmers are competing for a given
amount of land in each concentric ring. The result: agriculture is arrayed in a predictable ring structure, land rents
decline from the center along a predictable bid-rent curve,
and—big surprise—the market outcome is the efficient
allocation.

A currently popular buzzword among some scientists is
"emergence"—a fuzzy term referring to the idea that simple rules of individual behavior may produce quite complex aggregate outcomes that were not obviously built into
those rules, but that these complex outcomes may in turn
exhibit surprising underlying order. Well, guess what: the
von Thünen model is a spectacular example of emergence.
Where was the idea of rings of activity built into the assumption of maximizing behavior by farmers? And yet it
turns out to be a hidden implication. Who would have
thought that the result of a free-for-all competition for land
can be represented as the solution of an aggregate minimization problem? And yet there it is—an unexpected organizing principle. If emergence really is the kind of deep
insight that some people now claim, then von Thünen had
that insight a century and a half before it became fashion-
able. And indeed neoclassical economics can be regarded
as one of the pioneering sciences of emergence.

Now of course the von Thünen model, like the bulk
of economic models between 1820 and 1970, focused on
the case of perfect competition and constant returns. In
this case the market outcome is also the efficient plan. This
will not always be true. But there is nothing about the
economist's method that necessarily restricts it to examining perfect markets and efficient outcomes. It's true that

perfect-market models are easier to build, but the same methods applied to imperfect markets can also produce striking and unexpected insights.

But, you may ask, why restrict ourselves to these particular building blocks? Why, in particular, must economic reasoning be based on the assumption of self-interested, rational behavior? Why can't we build models based on more realistic psychological premises, or on a more historically based understanding of institutions? Or why can't we take into account the fact that tastes and motives are themselves socially determined, and build a field of "socioeconomics?"

I don't have any fundamental answer to these questions. In the long run we may suppose that economics will be part of an integrated social science, just as genetics has become a branch of biochemistry, which in turn is understood in principle if not often in practice to be grounded in quantum mechanics. Indeed, in the very longest run *every-thing* will be grounded in quantum mechanics. As an empirical proposition, however, attempts to find alternatives to the economist's formula of self-interest plus interaction—or, to use the title of a marvelous book by Thomas Schelling, *Micromotives and Macrobehavior*—have been notably unsuccessful.

Consider, for example, the repeated efforts of heterodox economic thinkers to find alternatives to the rational, profit-maximizing firm—like John Kenneth Galbraith's claim that modern corporations are in the hands, not of their stockholders, but of a "technostructure" driven by bureaucratic imperatives. Did these attempts lead anywhere? Surely the answer is no: once you get past the impressive-sounding neologisms, theories like Galbraith's make few useful predictions; and what he claimed as deep insights, like the insulation of managers from stockholders, turned out to be fragile observations that ceased to be true almost as soon as he made them. It is, of course, true that corporate managers do not always act in the interests of stockholders; but to the extent we have made any progress in thinking about that fact, it is through hard thinking about the principal-agent problem—which is simply an elaboration of the basic economistic emphasis on self-interested behavior.

In other words, *Homo economicus* is an implausible caricature, but a highly productive one, and no useful alternative has yet been found.

It is also the case that many of those who criticize mainstream economics for its narrowness don't understand what the field is or can do. At the crudest level, they simply have no idea what economics is about: Jay Forrester, founder of system dynamics, once replied to an economist who criticized his work by asserting that "Nordhaus, like all economists, only thinks in terms of one-way causation—he doesn't understand that variables may simultaneously affect each other." At a higher level, the idea of emergence is lost on most people who have not studied economics; the idea that markets can sometimes be a decentralized way of achieving efficient outcomes is seen as a sort of blind prejudice, not the deep insight about emergent properties that it is. At the most sophisticated level, critics think that perfect competition and perfect markets are all that economics can do.

I've already tried to describe how it is possible to use the basic self-interest-plus-interaction method of economics to make sense of seemingly heterodox ideas in development and geography; I'll want to talk more about the implications of that work shortly. But let me first ask why, despite all that I have said, some thinkers end up turning their back on the whole enterprise of modeling—or so they think.

Models and Metaphors

Many of those who reject the idea of economic models are ill-informed or even (perhaps unconsciously) intellectually dishonest. Still, there are highly intelligent and objective thinkers who are repelled by simplistic models for a much better reason: they are very aware that the act of building a model involves loss as well as gain. Africa isn't empty, but the act of making accurate maps can get you into the habit of imagining that it is. Model-building, especially in its early stages, involves the evolution of ignorance as well as knowledge; and someone with powerful intuition, with a deep sense of the complexities of reality, may well feel that from his point of view more is lost than is gained.

The problem is that there is no alternative to models. We all think in simplified models, all the time. The sophisticated thing to do is not to pretend to stop, but to be self-conscious—to be aware that your models are maps rather than reality.

There are many intelligent writers on economics who are able to convince themselves—and sometimes large numbers of other people as well—that they have found a way to transcend the narrowing effect of model-building. Invariably they are fooling themselves. If you look at the writing of anyone who claims to be able to write about social issues without stooping to restrictive modeling, you will find that his insights are based essentially on the use of metaphor. And metaphor is, of course, a kind of heuristic modeling technique.

In fact, we are all builders and purveyors of unrealistic simplifications. Some of us are self-aware: we use our models as metaphors. Others, including people who are indisputably brilliant and seemingly sophisticated, are sleepwalkers: they unconsciously use metaphors as models.

Now of course some people are better sleepwalkers than others. The metaphors of some anti-modelers stand up very well to the test of time—Hirschman's *Strategy of Economic Development*, for example, remains very readable and suggestive even today. For the most part, however, economic thinkers who imagine that they have broadened their vision by abandoning the effort to make simple models have done no such thing. All that they have really done is to use high-flown rhetoric to disguise, not least from themselves, their lack of clear understanding.

One good indicator of the perils of imagining that you can do best by avoiding a specific model is the frequency with which nonmodelers fall into crude fallacies. Look, for example, at any of the many writers on "competitiveness" whose compelling rhetoric masks a failure to understand that the trade balance is, *by definition*, equal to the difference between saving and investment; or who advocate targeting of "high-value-added" industries without stopping to ask why markets have not competed away that high value, and thus failed to notice that in practice industries with high value added per worker are capital-intensive sectors like oil refining, not high technology sectors like computers.

So modeling, which may seem simplistic, is in practice often a discipline that helps you avoid being even more simplistic. But there is more: a formal model, which may seem like a ridiculously stylized sketch of reality, will often suggest things that you would never think of otherwise. Consider, for example, the case of development theory.

The Fall and Rise of Development Theory, Again

Let me turn, once again, to the story of high development theory I introduced in the first lecture. By the late 1950s, as I have argued, high development theory was in a difficult position. Mainstream economics was moving in the direction of increasingly formal and careful modeling. While this trend was clearly overdone in many instances, it was an unstoppable and ultimately an appropriate direction of change. But it was difficult to model high development theory more formally, because of the problem of dealing with market structure.

The response of some of the most brilliant high development theorists, above all Albert Hirschman, was simply to opt out of the mainstream. They would build a new development school on suggestive metaphors, institutional realism, interdisciplinary reasoning, and a relaxed attitude toward internal consistency. The result was some wonderful writing, some inspiring insights, and (in my view) an intellectual dead end. High development theory simply faded out. A constant-returns, perfect-competition view of reality took over the development literature, and eventually via the World Bank and other institutions much of real-world development policy as well.

And yet in the end it turned out that mainstream economics eventually *did* find a place for high development theory. Like the Norwegians who discovered that the shapes of clouds do mean something, mainstream economics discovered that as its modeling techniques became more sophisticated, some neglected insights could be brought back in. And it was not simply a matter of rediscovery: the restatement of high development theory, in terms of such models as the Murphy et al. version of the Big Push, is not only clearer but in some ways deeper than the original statement.

First of all, the new models show that it is possible to tell high development-style stories in the form of a rigorous model. The methods of mainstream economics may have created a predisposition to constant returns, perfect competition models, but they need not be restricted to such models.

Second, these models, like Fultz's dishpan, show that the essential logic of high development stories emerges even in a highly simplified setting. It is common for those who haven't tried the exercise of making a model to assert that underdevelopment traps must necessarily result from some complicated set of factors—irrationality or short-sightedness on the part of investors, cultural barriers to change, inadequate capital markets, problems of information and learning, and so on. Perhaps these factors play a role, perhaps they don't: what we now know is that a low-level trap can arise with rational entrepreneurs, without so much as a whiff of cultural influences, in a model without capital, and with everyone fully informed.

Third, the models, unlike a purely verbal exposition, reveal the sensitivity of the conclusions to the assumptions. In particular, verbal expositions of the Big Push story make it seem like something that *must* be true. In models we see that it is something that *might* be true. A model makes one want to go out and start measuring, to see whether it looks at all likely in practice, whereas a merely rhetorical presentation gives one a false feeling of security in one's understanding.

Finally, models tells us something about what attitude is required to deal with complex issues in economics. Little models like the Murphy et al. Big Push may seem childishly simple, but I can report from observation that until they published their formalization of Rosenstein-Rodan, its conclusions were not obvious to many people, even those who have specialized in development. Economists tended to regard the Big Push story as essentially nonsensical—if modern technology is better, then rational firms would simply adopt it! (They missed the interaction between economies of scale and market size.) Non-economists tended to think that Big Push stories necessarily involved some rich interdisciplinary stew of effects, missing the simple core. In other words, economists were locked in their traditional models, non-economists were lost in the fog that results when you have no explicit models at all.

How did Murphy et al. break through this wall of confusion? Not by trying to capture the richness of reality, either with a highly complex model or with the kind of lovely metaphors that seem to evade the need for a model. They did it instead by *daring to be silly*: by representing the world in a dishpan, to get at an essential point.

In the end, the formalization of the Big Push was so easy that one finds oneself wondering whether the long slump in development theory was really necessary. The model is so simple: three pages, two equations, and one diagram. It could, it seems, have been written as easily in 1955 as in 1989. What would have happened to development economics, even to economics in general, if someone had legitimized the role of increasing returns and circular causation with a neat model thirty-five years ago?

But it didn't happen, and perhaps couldn't. Those economists who were attracted to the idea of powerful simplifications were still absorbed in the possibilities of perfect competition and constant returns; those who were drawn to a richer view, like Hirschman, became impatient with the narrowness and seeming silliness of the economics enterprise.

That the story may have been preordained does not keep it from being a sad one. Good ideas were left to gather dust in the economics attic for more than a generation; great minds retreated to the intellectual periphery. It is hard to know whether economic policy in the real world would have been much better if high development theory had not decayed so badly, since the relationship between good economic analysis and successful policy is far weaker than we like to imagine. Still, one wishes things had played out differently.

The Exile of Economic Geography

The story of economic geography is a bit different from that of development theory. For one thing, the modeling is considerably harder. The Murphy et al. Big Push story looks like something that could have been done forty years ago, had anyone happened on the right way to think about the problem. The spatial model presented in the appendix does not—it requires a sort of layering of technical tricks developed piece by piece over the past twenty years, and at the end I rely on simulation exercises of a kind that have only become easy to do on a desktop in the last few years. And I should admit that not everyone thinks that I have solved the problem of how to do spatial economics, or even

necessarily made a valuable contribution, with this particular type of model.

Moreover, economic geographers did not reject modeling in the way that high development theorists did. When
they found that they could not produce models in which
macrobehavior could be explained from the interaction of
micromotives, they essentially settled for what they could
do: schematic descriptions of the data or organizing principles that made intuitive sense and/or seemed to fit the
facts fairly well, without having the kind of deeply satisfying logic of, say, the von Thünen model. Central-place theory, rank-size rules, gravity equations, market potential
analyses: these were certainly modeling efforts, even if
they did not go all the way to maximization and equilibrium. Admittedly, during the 1970s there was something of
an antimodel, antiquantitative backlash in economic geography, drawing slightly on Marx and more than you might
imagine on Derrida. (The giveaway turns out to be the
phrase "post-Fordism": if you see that, it means that you
are dealing with a member of the Derrida-influenced regu-
lation school—deconstructionist geography!) But the traditions I described in lecture 2 were hardly those of people
who were unwilling to think in terms of models.

So in the case of economic geography one wonders
whether mainstream economics deserves to be faulted for
an unnecessarily narrow view of what constitutes useful
theory. Suppose that there is a subject of great intrinsic importance—as cities and the location of production surely
are. And suppose that there is a body of thinking about
that subject that seems to make considerable sense, shed a
fair amount of empirical light, but that doesn't seem to be
something we are currently able to wrap up neatly into
fully specified micromotives-and-macrobehavior models.

Should we completely ignore that body of thinking? I don't think so, and it speaks badly of our profession that we are so narrow-minded.

I can't resist a parallel with another area of economics, the study of business cycles. Keynesian economics is, in a way, not too unlike regional science. It is a collection of plausible models without good microfoundations, like IS-LM, mixed in with empirical relationships that work very well even though we don't quite know why, like Okun's law, all leavened by a few areas like consumption behavior in which models with full maximizing behavior are the norm. Regional science, whatever its academic reception, always found a ready market in the real world. Similarly, a basically Keynesian macro continues, whatever its academic status, to be the workhorse of monetary and fiscal policymaking, of forecasting and policy assessment, in the real world of events.

So what should the academic economics profession do about this unsatisfying subject—admit that it is intellectually messy but continue to teach it pending a well-specified theory, or exile it on the grounds that it is not serious economics and restrict our macroeconomics classes to issues of hyperinflation and long-run growth? You know what I think: in the long run all of our models will be as neat as the von Thünen model, but in the long run. . .

And yet what a difference a clean model makes. Consider the way I presented the various traditions in spatial economics—with central-place theory, market potential, cumulative causation, and external economies as different ways of looking at the same process, in which firms are attracted to the markets and supplies they provide for each other. Did the proponents of these ideas see themselves as offering variants on a common theme? Not as far as I can tell. If you look at a typical textbook on location, like Dicken and Lloyd's *Location in Space*, or a survey like Michael Chisholm's *Regions in Recession and Resurgence*— both excellent books, by the way, which I have found very helpful—you will find each of these ways of looking at agglomeration treated under a separate heading, as in effect a disjoint set of ideas. Central-place theory is viewed as a static neoclassical construct, when it is surely inconsistent with the neoclassical assumption of perfect competition and hard to imagine occurring except via a dynamic process. Market potential appears in a section or chapter on demand; cumulative causation in a section or chapter on dynamics, often treated as something having to do with Keynesian economics and export multipliers. And external economies are stuck in yet another place, often in the discussion of Weber and the three-points problem. So the impression of a unified, sensible tradition in economic geography that I may have conveyed is partly a construct, perhaps even to a greater extent than my rosy backward look at high development theory: now that we have a model, we impose a coherence on ideas that may have been far less coherent at the time.

So the sad exile of economic geography also has no villains. One cannot fault the geographers for their failure to develop full maximization-and-equilibrium models— although one can perhaps complain about their failure to understand how far short of that ideal they were falling. And one can understand the reluctance of the mainstream economists to muddy the clarity of that mainstream with the somewhat murky modeling efforts of the geographers— although the unwillingness to grant even one page in a thousand to fairly sensible efforts to make sense of an important subject seems extreme. And as with development theory, I believe that there will be a happy ending: in the end, we will integrate spatial issues into economics through clever models (preferably but not necessarily mine) that make sense of the insights of the geographers in a way that meets the standards of the economists.

Concluding Thoughts

One would like to draw some morals from these stories of ideas lost and found. It is easy to give facile advice. For those who are impatient with modeling and prefer to strike out on their own into the richness that an uninhibited use of metaphor seems to open up, the advice is to stop and think. Are you sure that you really have such deep insights that you are better off turning your back on the cumulative discourse among generally intelligent people that is modern economics? But of course you are.

And for those, like me, who basically try to understand the world through the metaphors provided by models, the advice is not to let important ideas slip by just because they haven't been formulated your way. Look for the folk wisdom on clouds—ideas that come from people who do not write formal models but may have rich insights. There may be some very interesting things out there. Strangely, though, I can't think of any.

The truth is, I fear, that there's not much that can be done about the kind of apparent intellectual waste that took place during the fall and rise of development economics or during the long intellectual exile of economic geography. A temporary evolution of ignorance, a period when our insistence on looking in certain directions leaves us unable to see what is right under our noses, may be the price of progress, an inevitable part of what happens when we try to make sense of the world's complexity.

Appendix

In lecture 2, I concluded by alluding to recent modeling work of mine that seems both to validate and to integrate several of the "outcast" traditions in economic geography: central-place theory, the market potential approach, and the idea of circular and cumulative causation. In this appendix I present the basic model that I have been using to explore these traditions. Parts of this approach have been published elsewhere; I first examined a two-location version of the model in Krugman (1991), explored the possibilities of a single-city economy and showed the usefulness of the market potential approach in Krugman (1993b), and showed how cumulative processes can lead to an approximate central-place outcome in Krugman (1993a). Here I offer an integrated treatment, of which all of these results can be seen as special cases.

While the model is simple in conception, and the results we get are quite intuitive, sometimes the dynamic analysis defies paper-and-pencil analytics. Thus the approach relies heavily on numerical examples. This is currently an unfashionable theoretical technique, but as we will see it is highly productive in this case.

The Basic Approach

Any interesting model of economic geography must exhibit a tension between two kinds of forces: "centripetal"
forces that tend to pull economic activity into agglomerations, and "centrifugal" forces that tend to break up such
agglomerations or limit their size.

There is a well-developed literature in urban economics,
largely deriving from the work of Henderson (1974), in
which a system of cities evolves from such a tension. In
Henderson-type models, the centripetal force arises from
assumed localized external economies in production; the
centrifugal force is urban land rent. Together with assumptions about the process of city formation, Henderson's approach yields a model of the number and sizes of cities
(though not of their location relative to one another).

There is a variant of this approach, represented for example by Fujita (1988), in which external economies are not
assumed but instead derived from increasing returns in a
monopolistically competitive industry producing non-
traded inputs. This leaves the basic approach unchanged,
and still leaves the spatial relationship of cities to each
other undetermined.

In my own work, I have tried a somewhat different
approach. No special assumptions are made either about localized external economies or nontradeability. Indeed, cities
are not primitive concepts in the model. Instead,
agglomerations emerge from the interaction between increasing returns at the level of the individual production
facility transportation costs, and factor mobility. Because of
increasing returns, it is advantageous to concentrate production of each good at a few locations. Because of transporta-

tion costs, the best locations are those with good access to markets (backward linkage) and suppliers (forward linkage). But access to markets and suppliers will be best precisely at those points at which producers have concentrated, and hence drawn mobile factors of production to their vicinity.

But not all factors are mobile, and the presence of immobile factors provides the centrifugal force that works against agglomeration. In principle, one should include urban land rents as part of the story; in the models I have worked out so far, however, this force is disregarded. Instead, the only force working against agglomeration is the incentive to set up new facilities to serve a dispersed agricultural hinterland.

Many of the elements of this story have been familiar to geographers for some time. (Useful surveys of the geography literature may be found in Dicken and Lloyd [1990] and Chisholm [1990].) As suggested in lecture 2, we may identify three main strands of "outcast" literature that bear on the approach taken here.

Closest in spirit to this model is the literature on "market potential," begun by Harris (1954). This literature argues that the desirability of a location as a production site depends on its access to markets, and that the quality of that access may be described by an index of "market potential," which is a weighted sum of the purchasing power of all locations, with the weights depending inversely on distance. Thus if Y_k is the income of location k, and D_{jk} is the distance between j and k, then the market potential of location j would be determined by an index of the form

$$M_j = \sum_k Y_k g(D_{jk}),\tag{1}$$

where $g(.)$ is some declining function.

Harris showed that the traditional manufacturing belt in the United States was, for a variety of $g(.)$ functions, the area of highest market potential; while he did not have an explicit model, he noted informally that the persistence of that belt could be attributed to the circular relationship in which industrial concentration tended both to follow and to create market access: "[M]anufacturing has developed partly in areas or regions of largest markets and in turn the size of these markets has been augmented and other favorable conditions have been developed by the very growth of this industry" (Harris 1954, p. 315, quoted by Chisholm 1990.)

Market potential analyses have been a staple of geographical discussion, especially in Europe (see, for example, Keeble et al. 1982). The main theoretical weakness of the approach is a lack of microeconomic foundations: while it is plausible that some index of market potential should help determine production location, there is no explicit representation of how the market actually works.

A second, closely related literature emphasizes the role of cumulative processes in regional growth. Pred (1966), drawing on the ideas of Myrdal (1957), suggested that agglomerations, by providing a large local market, are able to attract new industries, which further enlarges their local market, and so on. Other authors, such as Dixon and Thirlwall (1975), have proposed alternative motives for agglomeration but similar dynamics. Such cumulative causation suggests that initial advantages due to historical accident may play a major role in explaining the pattern of location. Like the market potential literature, however, the cumulative process literature lacks microfoundations.

Finally, we must mention central-place theory. Developed by Christaller (1933) and Lösch (1940), this theory emphasizes the trade-off between economies of scale and transportation costs. Central-place theory suggests that the attempts of firms to make the best of this trade-off should lead to the emergence of a lattice of production sites roughly evenly spaced across the landscape, perhaps in a hierarchical structure in which activities with larger scale economies or lower transport costs are concentrated in a smaller number of higher-level sites. Central-place theory has been a powerful organizing principle for research, even though it has well-known weaknesses. Most notably, not only does it not have any explicit microfoundations, it also neglects the circular causation that is such a central theme in both the market potential and the cumulative process literatures. Nonetheless, one would like a geographical model to exhibit at least some central-place features.

In summary, then, the urban economics literature offers clear and explicit analysis, but does not model the spatial relationship of cities to each other. The geographical tradition, while rich in insight, lacks a microeconomic foundation and as a result lacks the sharp edges we want from a theoretical analysis. What we want to do next is introduce a formal model, with complete microfoundations, that captures and clarifies the insights of the geography tradition.

Assumptions of the Model

In any model in which increasing returns play a crucial role, one must somehow handle the problem of market structure. Traditional urban models do so by assuming that increasing returns are purely external to firms, allowing the modeler to continue to assume perfect competition. The approach taken here, however, involves avoiding any direct assumption of external economies: externalities *emerge* as a consequence of market interactions involving economies of scale at the level of the individual firm. Thus we must somehow model an imperfectly competitive market structure. The workhorse model of this kind is, of course, the Dixit-Stiglitz (1977) model of monopolistic competition. Dixit-Stiglitz monopolistic competition is grossly unrealistic, but it is tractable and flexible; as we will see, it leads to a very special but very suggestive set of results.

We assume, then, an economy in which there are two sectors, manufacturing and agriculture. Everyone shares the same Cobb-Douglas tastes for the two types of goods:

$$U = C_M^\mu C_A^{1-\mu} \tag{2}$$

where μ is the share of manufactured goods in expenditure.

We assume that there is a single, homogeneous agricultural good. Manufactures, however, is a composite of a large number of symmetric product varieties, with a constant elasticity of substitution s between any two varieties:

$$C_M = \left[\sum_i c_i^{\frac{\sigma-1}{\sigma}} \right]^{\frac{\sigma}{\sigma-1}}, \tag{3}$$

In setting up the production side of this economy, we want to make allowance for both mobile and immobile factors of production, which at any given time are distributed across a number of locations $j = 1, \ldots, J$. One might suppose that the natural thing would be to assume that labor and possibly capital are the mobile factors, while land is the immobile factor; and that both mobile and immobile factors are used in both sectors. To do this, however, we would have to take account of land-labor substitution in both sectors, a major complication of the model. We would also have to worry about where landowners live. It turns out to be much simpler, if even less realistic, to assume that the two factors of production are both "labor": mobile "workers" who produce manufactured goods and immobile "farmers" who produce the agricultural good.

Farming is an activity that takes place under constant returns to scale; thus the farm labor used in producing any given quantity of the agricultural good at location j can, by choice of units, be set equal to production:

$$L_{Aj} = Q_{Aj}. \tag{4}$$

Manufacturing, however, we assume to involve economies of scale, with a fixed cost for any variety produced at any given location:

$$L_{Mij} = \alpha + \beta Q_{Mij}. \tag{5}$$

Let L_A and L_M represent the economywide supplies of the two factors "farmers" and "workers" respectively. We will assume that these supplies are fixed. They are, however, allocated across locations. A share ϕ_j of the farm labor force is in location j; we take these shares as exogenous. At any point in time, a share λ_j of the manufacturing labor force is also in location j; these shares will evolve over time in a fashion specified below.

At any point in time, then, there will be location-by-location full employment equations for both factors/sectors:

$$L_{Aj} = \phi_j L_A. \tag{6}$$

$$\sum_i L_{Mij} = \lambda_j L_M. \tag{7}$$

Next we introduce transportation costs. For simplicity, we make some completely unrealistic assumptions about these costs. First, we assume that they apply only to manufactured goods. Second, we assume that they take the "iceberg" form introduced by Paul Samuelson: instead of modeling a separate transportation industry, we simply assume that a fraction of any manufactured good shipped melts away en route. Specifically, let x be the amount of some good shipped from j to k, and let z be the amount that arrives; then we assume

$$z_{ijk} = e^{-\tau D_{jk}} x_{ijk'} \tag{8}$$

where τ is the transportation cost and D_{jk} is the distance between the two locations.

Finally, we turn to factor mobility. Farmers are assumed completely immobile. Workers are assumed to move toward locations that offer them higher real wages. (No attempt is made here to model the moving decision explicitly.) As we will see in the next section, it is possible to solve the model at any point in time for the real wages ω_j paid to workers at each location. Let us define the average real wage as

$$\overline{\omega} = \sum_j \lambda_j \omega_j. \tag{9}$$

Then the assumed law of motion of the economy is

$$\frac{d\lambda_j}{dt} = \rho \lambda_j (\omega_j - \overline{\omega}). \tag{10}$$

That is, workers move away from locations with below-average real wages and toward sites with above-average real wages.

We have now specified a complete model of geographic dynamics. The inputs into this model are the parameters μ, τ, and σ (which turn out to be the only parameters that cannot be eliminated by choice of units); a given allocation of farm labor across locations; a matrix of distances between locations; and an initial allocation of workers across locations. These inputs determine equilibrium at a point in time, and in particular the vector of real wages, which dictates the changes in the allocation of workers, leading to an evolution of that equilibrium over time.

This sounds pretty abstract. Our next step is to describe some of the features of short-run equilibrium.

Short-Run Equilibrium

As a preliminary step to the description of short-run equilibrium, it is useful to recall two basic points about Dixit-Stiglitz-type models.

First, in these models, the producer of any one manufactured variety faces a constant elasticity of demand σ. Her profit-maximizing strategy is therefore to set price as a fixed markup over marginal cost:

$$p_{ij} = \frac{\sigma}{\sigma - 1} \beta w_j, \tag{11}$$

where w_j is the wage rate of workers at location j.

By choice of units we can simply say that the f.o.b. price of manufactured goods at j is equal to the wage rate:

$$p_j = w_j. \tag{12}$$

Second, if firms are free to enter until profits are zero, there is a unique zero-profit output of any manufactured variety, which can be shown to be

$$Q_{Mi} = \frac{\alpha}{\beta}(\sigma - 1). \tag{13}$$

Since all varieties are produced at the same scale, the number of varieties produced at any given location is simply proportional to that location's manufacturing labor force. In particular, let n be the number of manufactured varieties produced in the economy as a whole, and let n_j be the number produced at location j. Then we have

$$n_j/n = \lambda_j. \tag{14}$$

Equation (14) plays a crucial role in the whole analysis in this approach. The logic of the model depends crucially on increasing returns, yet as we write out the equations of short-run equilibrium these increasing returns will not be very visible. Where did they go? The answer is that they are hidden in (14). What increasing returns do is to make it profitable to produce each variety in only one location, so that different locations do not produce the same set of goods but differentiated bundles of products. When a location gains labor it does not produce more of the same mix of products, but adds new products. This "quantization" of production is the only way in which increasing returns actually enter the solution, but it is enough: as we will see, the micro assumption does indeed have major macro effects.

There are now several ways to proceed. The one that seems easiest represents short-run equilibrium as the solution of four sets of equations.

First, we determine income at each location. Given our assumption of zero transport costs on agricultural goods, the wage rate of farmers is the same at all locations. Let there be μ workers and $1 - \mu$ farmers, a normalization that will set economywide income equal to 1; and let us measure all prices and wages in terms of the agricultural good. Then we have

$$Y_j = (1 - \mu)\phi_j + \mu\lambda_j w_j. \tag{15}$$

Next, we find the true or ideal price index of the manufactures aggregate to consumers at each location. To do this, we note that in order to have one unit of a manufactured variety make it from k to j, $\exp(\tau D_{jk})$ units must be shipped, so the c.i.f. price on arrival is $w_k \exp(\tau D_{jk})$. Given the CES function (3), the true price index of manufactures at j is therefore

$$T_j = \left[\sum_k \lambda_k (w_k e^{\tau D_{jk}})^{1-\sigma}\right]^{\frac{1}{\sigma-1}}. \tag{16}$$

Given these true price indices, we can solve for equilibrium wage rates. It can be shown that

$$w_j = \left[\sum_k Y_k (T_k e^{-\tau D_{jk}})^{\sigma-1}\right]^{\frac{1}{\sigma}} \tag{17}$$

It is worth stopping briefly at this point, to note that the right-hand side of (17) bears a family resemblance to the market potential index (1). Like that index, it depends on a weighted sum of purchasing power at all locations, with the weights inversely related to distance. The difference is that the true price indices also enter into the index; essentially this reflects the effect of competition from producers in other locations, which is missing from the usual market potential approach. But there is a definite affinity between the workings of this model and the market potential tradition in geography.

Equation (17), however, only determines wage rates in terms of agricultural goods. Workers are interested in real wages in terms of a consumption basket that includes manufactures as well. Thus the real wage depends on both the wage in terms of the agricultural good and on the manufactures price index:

$$\omega_j = w_j T_j^{-\mu}. \tag{18}$$

We now have a soluble set of equations for short-run equilibrium. Equations (15)–(17) need to be solved simultaneously for the vectors Y, T, and w; given these one can then solve (18).

These equations are easily solved on the computer—in the numerical examples below, I simply started with an initial guess at w and then cycled (with some damping) over (15)–(17) until convergence. In general, however, they cannot be solved with pencil and paper. Yet we would like to get some intuition about the forces in our model before going over to numerical methods.

In order to do this, we examine a limited question for a special case, before moving on to more general problems.

Centripetal and Centrifugal Forces

In this section of the appendix I ask a question originally posed in Krugman (1991), but which we can now restate in terms of our more general framework.

Consider an economy with only two locations, each of which has the same number of farmers ($\phi_1 = \phi_2 = 0.5$). Under what conditions is concentration of all manufacturing in one location ($\lambda_1 = 1$ or 0) an equilibrium? By answering this question, we get some useful insights into how the parameters of the model affect the relative strength of centripetal and centrifugal tendencies.

What we do is solve (15)–(18) on the assumption that $\lambda_1 = 1$, $\lambda_2 = 0$ (the case where $\lambda_1 = 0$ is symmetric). We ask whether, in that case, the real wage that workers would earn at location 2 is less than that at location 1. Concentration of manufacturing at 1 is an equilibrium if and only if $\omega_2 < \omega_1$ in that case.

To save notation, let's normalize the distance between the two locations to 1. Then we immediately find from (15)–(18) that

$$w_1 = T_1 = \omega_1 = 1, \tag{19}$$

and, substituting, that

$$\omega_2 = \left[\frac{1+\mu}{2}e^{-\tau(\sigma-1)} + \frac{1-\mu}{2}e^{\tau(\sigma-1)}\right]^{1/\sigma}, \tag{20}$$

and

$$\omega_2 = e^{-\tau\mu}\left[\frac{1+\mu}{2}e^{-\tau(\sigma-1)} + \frac{1-\mu}{2}e^{\tau(\sigma-1)}\right]^{1/\sigma}. \tag{21}$$

The condition for sustainability of concentrated manufacturing, then, is that the right-hand side of (21) be less than one.

In the intuitive discussion of agglomeration in the first part of this appendix, it was argued that agglomeration is possible because of the circular relationship between the location of the market and the location of manufacturing. We can see this intuition borne out in this model by considering what would happen if manufacturing were a very small part of the economy, μ close to zero. Then (21) would reduce to

$$\omega_2 = \left[\frac{1}{2}e^{-\tau(\sigma-1)} + \frac{1}{2}e^{\tau(\sigma-1)}\right]^{\frac{1}{\sigma}} < 1, \tag{22}$$

which is always less than one because of Jensen's inequality. In this case, in which firms sold only to the agricultural market, it would always be advantageous to move *away* from any concentration of manufacturing in order to get away from competitors.

This desire to get away from competition represents the centrifugal force in this model, the force that works against agglomeration. By examining (21), however, we see that when the manufacturing sector is a significant part of the economy there are two centripetal forces working to hold an agglomeration together. First, the first term in (21) becomes less than one. By referring back to (18), we see that this term is there because of the role of manufacturing firms as suppliers of goods to manufacturing workers; in effect, this is a kind of Hirschman (1958)-type *forward linkage*. Second, the expression inside the brackets involves a higher weight on the component that is less than one and a lower weight on the component that is greater than one. This reflects the point that the location in which manufacturing is concentrated has a higher income than the other location. Thus there is also a *backward linkage* in which manufacturing wants to be close to the market that manufacturing itself creates.

An economy with a large μ, then, may have a self-sustaining manufacturing concentration due to forward and backward linkages, and we may presume that concentration is more likely, the larger is μ. What about the other parameters?

The parameter whose effect may seem counterintuitive to some readers is the transportation cost τ. Concentration is more likely when transport costs are *low*. To see why, we note the following:

First, when $\tau = 0$, $\omega_2 = 1$. No surprise here: in the absence of transport costs, location doesn't matter.

Second, in the vicinity of $\tau = 0$, we find that

$$\frac{\partial \omega_2}{\partial \tau} = -\mu - \frac{\sigma - 1}{\sigma}\mu < 0. \tag{23}$$

Finally, we note that (21) may be rewritten as

$$\omega_2 = \left[\frac{1 + \mu}{2} e^{-\tau(2\sigma - 1)} + \frac{1 - \mu}{2} e^{\tau[(\sigma - 1) - \sigma\mu]} \right]^{1/\sigma}. \qquad (24)$$

If

$$\frac{\sigma - 1}{\sigma} > \mu, \qquad (25)$$

then as τ grows the real wage in location 2 eventually must exceed 1. In that case the relationship between transport costs and the real wage must have the shape illustrated by the curve in figure A.1. At high transport costs a concentration of production is not sustainable; there is a range of low transport costs for which such a concentration is not sustainable.

If (25) is not satisfied, the curve lies below 1 for *all* values of τ. To understand this case, we note that $\sigma/(\sigma-1)$ is the ratio of price and hence average cost to marginal cost, a measure of equilibrium economies of scale. Thus (25) amounts to saying that neither the share of manufacturing in the economy nor economies of scale are too large. If scale economies and the manufacturing share are sufficiently large, workers will prefer to cluster together even with prohibitive transport costs.

Returning to the case where (25) is satisfied, we note that what we have defined is a critical value of τ, τ^*, below which concentration is an equilibrium. We may offer some rough intuition here by stepping a bit outside the formal model. Basically, when transport costs are sufficiently low it is worthwhile for manufacturers to concentrate their production geographically so as to realize economies of scale. Once they have decided to concentrate production, however, the optimal location is one that other producers

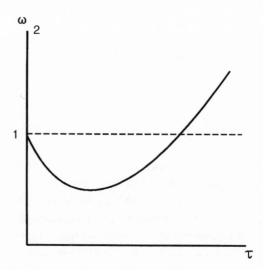

Figure A.1

have also chosen. So low transport costs foster agglomeration.

One might expect that concentration would also be more likely the higher is μ. It is straightforward to show (see Krugman 1991) that

$$\frac{\partial \tau^*}{\partial \mu} > 0. \tag{26}$$

Let us also bear in mind that σ, the elasticity of substitution, is inversely related to the equilibrium degree of economies of scale. Thus we would expect to find that a high elasticity of substitution works against agglomeration, and we can indeed show (again see Krugman 1991) that

$$\frac{\partial \tau^*}{\partial \sigma} < 0. \tag{27}$$

What we get from this static exercise is an indication of how the parameters of the model ought to affect the balance between the centripetal forces that favor agglomeration and the centrifugal forces that oppose it. Agglomeration is favored by low transport costs (low τ), a large share of manufacturing in the economy (high μ) and strong economies of scale at the level of the firm (low σ).

This is, however, only an analysis of a static, two-location equilibrium. We now turn to dynamics in a multi-location example.

Dynamics in a Multi-Location Model: The Economy as a Self-Organizing System

We now turn to a dynamic, multi-location model. In doing so we find that paper-and-pencil analysis will no longer suffice, and must be supplemented with numerical methods. Since the model has only a few parameters, however, it is not hard to use numerical methods to explore its properties fairly thoroughly; and the numerical results are easy to understand given the intuition developed in the two-location case.

We assume, then that there are $J > 2$ locations, and we return to the assumption that agricultural workers are equally distributed among the locations, with a share $1/J$ in each.

In a many-location model it is necessary to specify the matrix of distances between locations. I choose the simplest setup that preserves symmetry: the locations are equally spaced around a circle, with transportation possible only along the circle's circumference. We let the distance between any two neighboring locations equal 1. In the numerical examples described shortly, we consider in particular the case of 12 locations, laid out like a clock face.

(The number 12 was chosen because it is a fairly small number with a large number of divisors.) In this case, the distance between location 2 and location 7 is 5; the distance between location 2 and location 11 is 3.

How can we explore this economy? I have adopted what we might call a Monte Carlo approach: start the economy with a random allocation of manufacturing workers across locations, and then let it evolve until it converges. We get insight into the model by performing this experiment repeatedly with various parameter values.

Consider first a base case (chosen after some experimenting) in which μ = .2, τ = .2, and σ = 4. Figure A.2 shows what happens on a typical run of this case. The first set of bars show the initial, random allocation of workers across locations, the second the eventual distribution. The initial random allocation of manufacturing eventually organizes itself into two manufacturing concentrations, at locations 6 and 11, that is, 5 apart. This puts the two concentrations almost but not exactly opposite one another on the circle.

There are several interesting points to notice here. First, it is evident that there is a process of reinforcement of initial advantage. Thus location 11, which starts with the largest share of workers, is able thereby to attract still more workers and eventually take half of the total. This is exactly the kind of cumulative process described by Pred (1966).

The process is not, however, simply one in which locations with larger initial workforces grow. A second city emerges at location 6. Now while 6 had a large initial labor force, it was actually smaller than that of other locations, for example location 10. But location 10 was too close to the winning location 11, and fell under its "agglomeration shadow," whereas 6 was able to match 11's eventual sta-

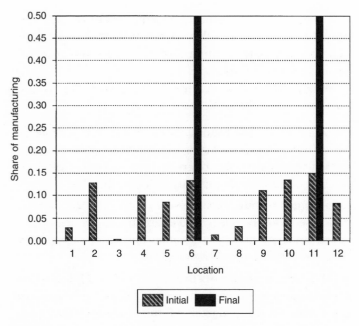

Figure A.2

tus thanks to its relative lack of rivals for its agricultural hinterland. This is why the two emergent cities are almost opposite one another—and therefore why the eventual pattern is one of two central places almost symmetrically placed.

Does this case always produce the same result? Not exactly. In the course of a number of runs with these parameter values, two concentrations 5 apart occurred about 60 percent of the time, two concentrations 6 apart occurred on almost all other occasions. At rare intervals a run would lead to 3 equally spaced concentrations.

Clearly the model economy shows multiple equilibria both in terms of which locations play which role and to some extent even in terms of the equilibrium spatial structure. Nonetheless, it is also clear that there is a systematic tendency toward formation of central places roughly evenly spaced across the landscape.

What happens if we change the parameters? I have tried runs on each of three alternative cases:

i. Less differentiated products ($\sigma = 2$, $\tau = .2$, $\mu = .2$): In this case (in which firms have more market power, and in which the equilibrium degree of scale economies is also larger), all runs produced only a single city.

ii. A larger manufacturing share ($\sigma = 4$, $\tau = .2$, $\mu = .4$): In this case, in which one would expect the backward and forward linkages driving agglomeration to be stronger, we also consistently get only a single city.

iii. Lower transport costs ($\sigma = 4$, $\tau = .1$, $\mu = .2$): In this case we would expect there to be less incentive to set up multiple urban centers, and again all runs produce only a single city.

What do we learn? We have already seen, earlier in the appendix, how both the market potential and cumulative process approaches are more or less validated in this model. Now we see not only that the same approach can produce multiple agglomerations, but that something resembling central-place theory also emerges, because the dynamic forces do tend to produce agglomerations that are roughly evenly spaced across the landscape.

Notes

Chapter 1

1. The reference is Craig Murphy, "The Evolution of Ignorance in European Mapping of Africa, 1500–1800, and the Case for Methodological Pluralism in International Studies," forthcoming in *Alternatives*.

2. It will become apparent that what I identify as "high development theory" is essentially the nexus among the external economy/balanced growth debate, the concept of linkages, and the surplus labor doctrine. This era began with Rosenstein-Rodan (1943) and more or less ended with Hirschman (1958). Obviously this nexus does not cover all of what was happening in the field of development economics even at that time, but it is the core of what I believe needs to be recaptured.

3. Actually four, if one counts the case where (2) is not satisfied, so that the economy actually produces less using modern techniques. In this case it clearly stays with the traditional methods.

Chapter 2

1. I am inspired to offer a variant on a standard economics joke. Two economists were walking down the hall when the younger of them noticed an interesting research topic. "Look," he said, "there's an interesting topic." "Nonsense," replied his colleague, "if it were really there someone would already have worked on it."

2. Regional scientists are both good-humored and frustrated by their failure to be taken seriously by economists proper. When I gave a sympathetic lecture at Penn's Regional Science Department, the students

presented me with a T-shirt adorned on the front with a picture of Walter Isard, and on the back with the logo, "Space: The Final Frontier."

3. Joel Garreau, the journalist who wrote the entertaining book *Edge City* about the new subcenters, has a revealing discussion of the conditions under which a subcenter really takes off. He says that when there are 10 million square feet of office space, the local market becomes large enough to support key services, in particular at least one luxury hotel, and that at that point growth becomes explosive. Doesn't this sound exactly like Pred's story about regional growth?

Chapter 3

1. This account is taken from Edward Lorenz's *The Essence of Chaos*.

References

Chisholm, M. 1990. *Regions in Recession and Resurgence*. London: Hyman.

Christaller, W. 1933. *Central Places in Southern Germany*. Jena: Fischer. English translation by C. W. Baskin. London: Prentice-Hall, 1966.

Dicken, P., and P. Lloyd. 1990. *Location in Space*. New York: Harper and Row.

Dixit, A., and J. Stiglitz. 1977. "Monopolistic Competition and Optimum Product Diversity." *American Economic Review* 67: 297–308.

Dixon, R., and A. P. Thirlwall. 1975. "A Model of Regional Growth Differences along Kaldorean Lines." *Oxford Economic Papers* 27, 201–214.

Fleming, J. M. 1955. "External Economies and the Doctrine of Balanced Growth." *Economic Journal* 65: 241–256.

Fujita, M. 1988. "A Monopolistic Competition Model of Spatial Agglomeration: Differentiated Product Approach." *Regional Science and Urban Economics* 18: 87–124.

Harris, C. 1954. "The Market as a Factor in the Localization of Industry in the United States." *Annals of the Association of American Geographers* 64: 315–348.

Henderson, J. V. 1974. "The Sizes and Types of Cities." *American Economic Review* 64: 640–656.

Hirschman, A. 1958. *The Strategy of Economic Development*. New Haven: Yale University Press.

Keeble, D. E., P. L Owens, and C. Thompson. 1982. "Regional Accessibility and Economic Potential in the European Community." *Regional Studies* 16: 419–432.

Krugman, P. 1991. "Increasing Returns and Economic Geography." *Journal of Political Economy* 99: 183–199.

Krugman, P. 1993a. "On the Number and Location of Cities." *European Economic Review* 37: 293–298.

Krugman, P. 1993b. "First Nature, Second Nature, and Metropolitan Location." *Journal of Regional Science* 33: 129–144.

Leibenstein, H. 1957. *Economic Backwardness and Economic Growth.* New York: Wiley.

Lewis, W. A. 1954. "Economic Development with Unlimited Supplies of Labor." *The Manchester School* 22: 139–191.

Lewis, W. A. 1955. *The Theory of Economic Growth.* London: Allen and Unwin.

Little, I. M. D. 1982. *Economic Development.* New York: Twentieth Century Fund.

Lorenz, E. 1993. *The Essence of Chaos.* Seattle: University of Washington Press.

Losch, A. 1940. *The Economics of Location.* Jena: Fischer. English translation, New Haven: Yale University Press, 1954.

Murphy, R., A. Shleifer, and R. Vishny. 1989. "Industrialization and the Big Push." *Journal of Political Economy* 97: 1003–1026.

Myrdal, G. 1957. *Economic Theory and Under-developed Regions.* London: Duckworth.

Nelson, R. 1956. "A Theory of the Low Level Equilibrium Trap in Underdeveloped Economies." *American Economic Review* 46: 894–908.

Pred, A. 1966. *The Spatial Dynamics of U.S. Urban-Industrial Growth.* Cambridge: MIT Press.

Rosenstein-Rodan, P. 1943. "Problems of Industrialization of Eastern and South-Eastern Europe." *Economic Journal* 53: 202–211.

Scitovsky, T. 1954. "Two Concepts of External Economies." *Journal of Political Economy* 62: 143–151.

Young, A. 1928. "Increasing Returns and Economic Progress." *Economic Journal* 38: 527–542.

Index